ॐ

# GAYATRI MANTRA in 108 writing



## A Phonetic TRANSLITERATION/TRANSCRIPTION for recitation

Ashwini Kumar Aggarwal

जय गुरुदेव

ISBN13: 978-93-92201-26-4 Paperback Edition
ISBN13: 978-93-92201-03-5 Hardbound Edition
ISBN13: 978-93-92201-11-0 Digital Edition



Title: **Gayatri Mantra in 108 writing scripts**
Author: **Ashwini Kumar Aggarwal**

Printed and Published by
**Devotees of Sri Sri Ravi Shankar Ashram**
34 Sunny Enclave, Devigarh Road,
Patiala 147001, Punjab, India

https://advaita56.weebly.com/
The Art of Living Centre

https://www.artofliving.org/

30th August 2021 Krishna Janmashtami, Bhadrapada Ashtami
Sarvartha Siddhi Yoga, Rohini Nakshatra, Varsha Ritu
Vikram Samvat 2078 Ananda, Saka Era 1943 Plava

1st Edition August 2021

जय गुरुदेव

## Dedication

# Sri Sri Ravi Shankar

who revived the meaning & effect of chanting & singing

## Blessing

Gā-ya-trī – there are three types of misery. We have three bodies, the gross body, the subtle and the causal body. And in all the three levels there is misery. The human life has to cross-over all the three, and that is what Gayatri means. One who sings it, sails over the ocean of misery to go to bliss.

*The Gayatri mantra is one of the greatest prayers mankind has.*

What does it say? Let me soak in the Divine, and let the Divine destroy all my sins. The Divine light that burns all sin, let me adore and soak in that Divine light. And let the Divinity inspire my intellect.

Sri Sri Ravi Shankar
Q & A in Bangalore Ashram, Aug 2, 2012

## Preface

Traditionally the Gayatri Mantra is initiated in the Yagnopavit ceremony, also called Upanayanam, by a Master to his disciples in a gurukul.

However, most of us learn this famed mantra through radio, our grandparents or our favorite smartphone.

What is the difference? In a gurukul when the guru gives this mantra, he ensures the intellect is receptive, respectful and compassionate in the use of the Mantra. INTELLECT governs CHARACTER & SUCCESS, and rules our entire LIFE.

Mantras are carefully chosen words strung like a gorgeous necklace in tuned verses. Specific words with deep meanings, they emanate powerful vibrations. The whole universe is नाम रूप - name & form – i.e. vibration. Scientifically, electrons and protons are spinning waves. When you chant, your tongue moves inside the mouth, touching the root, palate, lips or teeth, and stimulates the hypothalamus, pineal and pituitary glands, corresponding to the sahasrara and ajna chakras. The palate has 84 meridian points corresponding to the 84 Yoga asanas. The recitation sound wave strongly impinges the actions of the glands and thus governs the endocrine and circulatory systems, releasing necessary enzymes and assisting proper pulsation of the heart. Thus, the sound vibrations of mantra chanting help balance the body, mind and senses, and have immense immunizing and healing effects.

Often when we sit down to meditate, or to solve a complex equation, our emotions and sensations cause turbulences. Chanting helps by cooling the nervous system, reducing the flicker of the mind, and the mind gets soft and ready for Meditation and the Task at hand.

The 24 Syllabic Verse

The Gayatri Mantra is traditionally known as the verse consisting of 24 syllables i.e., 24 distinct sounds. These 24 syllables are arranged in triplets of 8 sounds as:

तत्[1] स[2]वि[3]तुर्[4] व[5]रे[6]ण्[7]यम्[8]
भर्[9]गो[10] दे[11]व[12]स्य[13] धी[14]म[15]हि[16]
धि[17]यो[18] यो[19] नः[20] प्र[21]चो[22]द[23]यात्[24]

tat[1] sa[2]vi[3]tur[4] va[5]re[6]ṇ[7]yam[8]
bhar[9]go[10] de[11]va[12]sya[13] dhī[14]ma[15]hi[16]
dhi[17]yo[18] yo[19] naḥ[20] pra[21]co[22]da[23]yāt[24]

Note[7] ण् (ṇ) for enunciation needs a vowel and the syllable is hence written as णि (ṇi) and it almost sounds like that.

Moreover, this verse is always prefixed additionally with:

| ॐ भूर् भुवः स्वः | oṃ bhūr bhuvaḥ svaḥ |
|---|---|

And thus the actual verse used in chanting or reading is then:

| ॐ भूर् भुवः स्वः | oṃ bhūr bhuvaḥ svaḥ |
|---|---|
| तत् सवितुर् वरेण्यम् | tat savitur vareṇyam |
| भर्गो देवस्य धीमहि | bhargo devasya dhīmahi |
| धियो यो नः प्रचोदयात् | dhiyo yo naḥ pracodayāt |

The Sun Mantra

Also known as the Savitri mantra (सावित्रि), in honor of the Sun (सवितृ), that is the de-facto life bestower and intellect governor for all denizens of planet Earth.

Notes in phonetic Transliteration

- The Latin script is transliterated using IAST.
- Anusvara (ṃ) and Visarga (ḥ) use the extended character set that has a dot below the letters m, h respectively.
- Most Indian languages that have native *anusvara* and *visarga* symbols are accordingly transliterated.
- However for languages or scripts where these symbols are not used, the anusvara is replaced with makara (m), and the visarga is replaced with hakara (h) in transliteration.
- Similarly, where the ॐ (Om/Aum) symbol is present, it is used; otherwise, the transliteration uses ओम् (om) or ओं (oṃ).
- The anusvara is a *sandhi* symbol caused by a makara. Written texts have the word वरेण्यम् as वरेण्यं, however we have preferred वरेण्यम् without the sandhi.
- In some cases, the text भुवः स्वः is phonetically arranged as भुवस् स्वह since that's what it sounds like when chanted.
- The full stop (double danda) is arbitrarily shown to prevent ambiguity.
- Lastly, it is stated that this is more or less a humble attempt, and lacking in fidelity for a few scripts.

# Contents

## 1. Devanagari

**ॐ भूर् भुवः स्वः**

**तत् सवितुर् वरेण्यम्**

**भर्गो देवस्य धीमहि**

**धियो यो नः प्रचोदयात्  ॥**

---

Devanagari is an abugida script, i.e., each consonant contains an inherent vowel. It is common in India for Hindi, Marathi, Sanskrit. It is used in Nepal for Nepali. Etymologically *deva-nagar-i = luminous city in*, i.e., used by people living in bright and creative workplaces, to achieve one's ultimate aim and get aligned to the supreme Divinity.

sung by Lata Mangeshkar -
https://www.youtube.com/watch?v=oTRU5Gwj0V4

**Quote** *"The Gayatri is a universal prayer enshrined in the Vedas. It is addressed to the Immanent and Transcendent Divine which has been given the name 'Savita,' meaning 'that from which all this is born.' The Gayatri may be considered as having three parts - (i) Adoration (ii) Meditation (iii) Prayer. First, the Divine is praised, then It is meditated upon in reverence and finally, an appeal is made to the Divine to awaken and strengthen the intellect, the discriminating faculty of man. The Gayatri is considered as the essence of the Vedas. Veda means knowledge, and this prayer fosters and sharpens the knowledge-yielding faculty. As a matter of fact, the four core-declarations enshrined in the four Vedas are implied in this Gayatri mantra."* **unquote**

Sri Sathya Sai Speaks, vol 13.34: June, 20, 1977

## 2. Latin (Roman/English)

oṃ bhūr bhuvaḥ svaḥ
tat savitur vareṇyam
bhargo devasya dhīmahi
dhiyo yo naḥ pracodayāt.

---

Roman or Latin script is common across Europe and America, New Zealand and Australia, and is also today the lingua franca of the planet. **The above shows mantra in English**.

### Latin (Roman/French)

oṃ bhūr bhuvaḥ svaḥ
tát savitúr váreṇyam
bhárgo devásya dhīmahi
dhíyo yó naḥ pracodáyāt.

---

The above shows mantra in **French** which has a slight change in **vowel acute accent** as compared to English.

### Latin (Roman/Spanish)

om bur buváj suáj
tat savitúr váreniam
bargo devásia dímaji
díio io naj prachodáiat.

---

The above shows mantra in **Spanish** which has a slight change in **phonetics** and vowel accents as compared to English.

# 3. Ahom

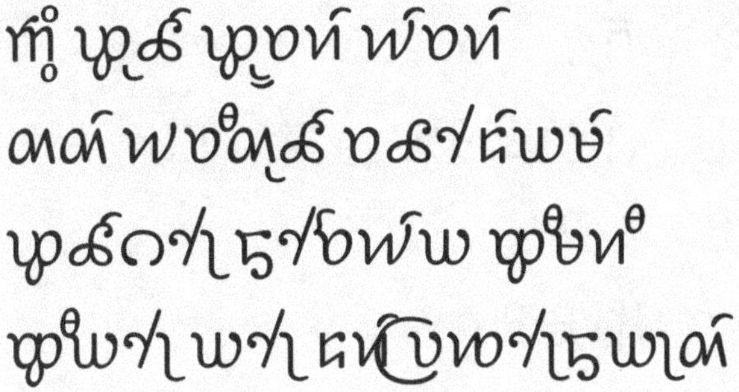

Used in the eastern state of Assam in India, Ahom was used by the Tai Ahom people who came from Burma and settled in India. It was later superseded by Assamese.

- Abugida (Mainland Southeast Asian)
- Languages – Tai
- People – Ahom-ese
- Places – Burma, Assam
- Related scripts – Brahmi, Old Burmese
- History – Brahmaputra valley circa 1250 to 1750 AD. Coins and bark manuscripts available
- Unicode block U+11700 - U+1174F

# 4. Amharic (Amara Fidel)

ዖን ቡሀ ቡቭ ጽቭኅ
ጥጥ ጽቪጡህ ቭሄኒይም
ብህኅ ደቭጽይ ዲምሂ
ዲዮ ዮ ንህ ፕህኮድይጥ

---

- Abugida (Language Family -Afro-Asian)
- Languages – Ethiopian, Semitic
- People – Amhara, Rastafari, Jewish
- Places – Ethiopia, Israel
- Related scripts – Ge’ez
- History – circa 1150 AD to present. Official language
- Unicode block U+1200 – U+137F

## 5. Ariyaka (Pali)

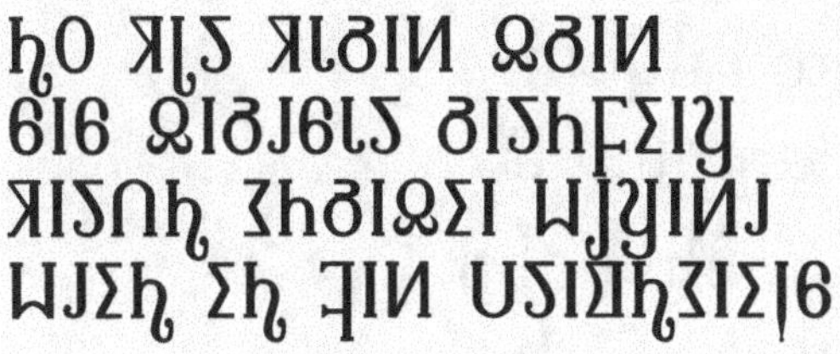

- Abugida
- Languages – Pali
- People – Thai, Buddhist
- Places – Siam, Thailand, Sri Lanka
- Related scripts – Pali, Khmer
- History – circa 1833 AD, reign of King Rama IV
- Unicode block - NONE
- http://www.skyknowledge.com/ariyaka.htm

# 6. Armenian (Western Armenian)

ոմ պհուր պհուվահ սվահ
դադ սավիդուր վարենյամ
պհարկո տևասյա տհīմահի

տհիյո յո նահ̣ բրաcոտայāդ

---

- Alphabet (Language Family -European)
- Languages – Armenian, Turkish, Kurdish
- People – Armenian
- Places – Armenia (former Soviet Union), Iran, Turkey
- Related scripts – Georgian
- History – circa 405 AD to present. Official language
- Unicode block U+ 0530 – U+058F

# 7. Balinese

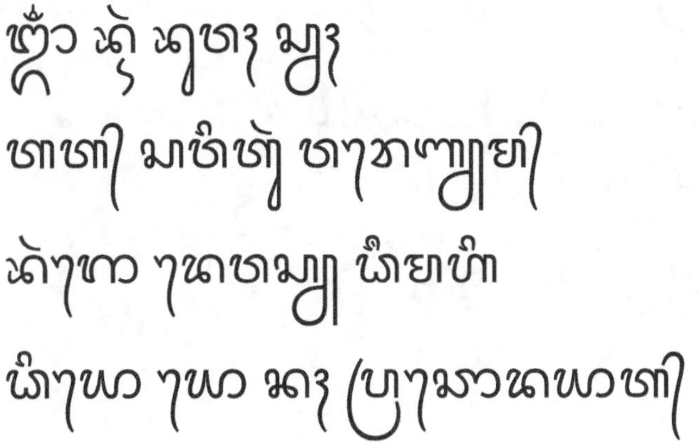

A descendent of Brahmi, this script is known as akshara bali अक्षर बालि (i.e., an alphabet to write what is spoken).

- Abugida (Insular Southeast Asian)
- Languages – Austronesian Balinese, Old Javanese, Sasak, Sanskrit
- People – Balinese
- Places – Bali (Indonesia)
- Related scripts – Brahmi, Javanese, Lontara
- History – circa 1000 AD to present. Official language
- Unicode block U+ 1B00 - U+1B7F

# 8. Bamum

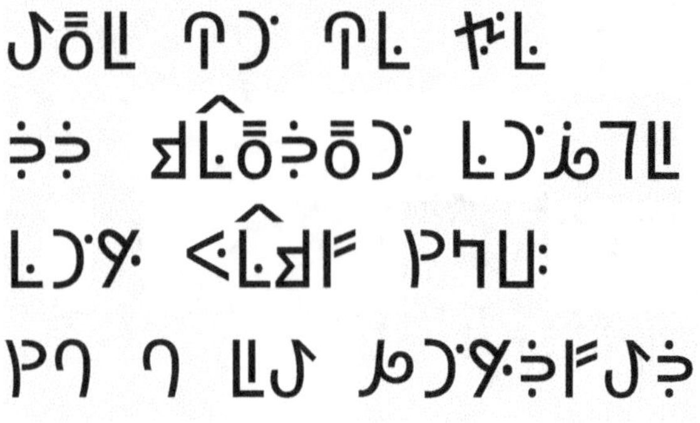

---

- Syllabary (African)
- Languages – Bamum
- People – Cameroonian
- Places – Cameroon (Africa)
- Related scripts – Bagam
- History – circa 1896 to 1931 AD
- Unicode block U+A6A0 – U+A6FF and Supplement U+16800 - U+16A3F

## 9. Bangla (Bengali)

ওঁ ভূর্ ভুবঃ স্বঃ
তত্ সবিতুর্ বরেণ্যম্
ভর্গো দেবস্য ধীমহি
ধিযো যো নঃ প্রচোদযাত্ ॥

---

Bangla or Bengali is the script of West Bengal in India. India's national song and anthem were originally written in Bangla. National Anthem by Nobel laureate Rabindranath Tagore.

জনগণমন-অধিনায়ক জয় হে ভারতভাগ্যবিধাতা!
পঞ্জাব সিন্ধু গুজরাট মরাঠা দ্রাবিড় উৎকল বঙ্গ বিন্ধ্য হিমাচল যমুনা গঙ্গা উচ্ছলজলধিতরঙ্গ তব শুভ নামে জাগে, তব শুভ আশিস মাগে, গাহে তব জয়গাথা। জনগণমঙ্গলদায়ক জয় হে ভারতভাগ্যবিধাতা! জয় হে, জয় হে, জয় হে, জয় জয় জয়, জয় হে॥ অহরহ তব আহ্বান প্রচারিত, শুনি তব উদার বাণী হিন্দু বৌদ্ধ শিখ জৈন পারসিক মুসলমান খৃস্টানী পূরব পশ্চিম আসে তব সিংহাসন-পাশে প্রেমহার হয় গাঁথা। জনগণ-ঐক্য-বিধায়ক জয় হে ভারতভাগ্যবিধাতা! জয় হে, জয় হে, জয় হে, জয় জয় জয়, জয় হে॥ পতন-অভ্যুদয়-বন্ধুর পন্থা, যুগ-যুগ ধাবিত যাত্রী। হে চিরসারথি, তব রথচক্রে মুখরিত পথ দিনরাত্রি। দারুণ বিপ্লব-মাঝে তব শঙ্খধ্বনি বাজে সঙ্কটদুঃখত্রাতা। জনগণপথপরিচায়ক জয় হে ভারতভাগ্যবিধাতা! জয় হে, জয় হে, জয় হে, জয় জয় জয় জয় হে॥ ঘোরতিমিরঘন নিবিড় নিশীথে পীড়িত মূর্ছিত দেশে জাগ্রত ছিল তব অবিচল মঙ্গল নতনয়নে অনিমেষে। দুঃস্বপ্নে আতঙ্কে রক্ষা করিলে অঙ্কে স্নেহময়ী তুমি মাতা। জনগণদুঃখত্রায়ক জয় হে ভারতভাগ্যবিধাতা! জয় হে, জয় হে, জয় হে, জয় জয় জয় জয় হে॥ রাত্রি প্রভাতিল, উদিল রবিচ্ছবি পূর্ব-উদয়গিরিভালে-গাহে বিহঙ্গম, পুণ্য সমীরণ নবজীবনরস ঢালে। তব করুণারুণরাগে নিদ্রিত ভারত জাগে তব চরণে নত মাথা। জয় জয় জয় হে, জয় রাজেশ্বর ভারতভাগ্যবিধাতা! জয় হে, জয় হে, জয় হে, জয় জয় জয় জয় হে॥

# 10. Bassa Vah (Vah)

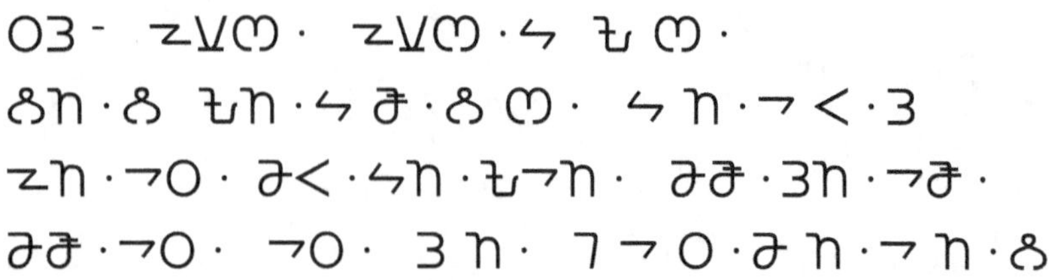

---

- Alphabet (African)
- Languages – Bassa, Kru, Niger-Congo
- People – Liberian
- Places – Liberia (Africa), Sierra Leone
- Related scripts – NA
- History – circa 500 BC, reinvented 1959 AD
- Unicode block U+16AD0 – U+16AFF
- https://r12a.github.io/scripts/bassavah/

# 11. Batak (surat Batak)

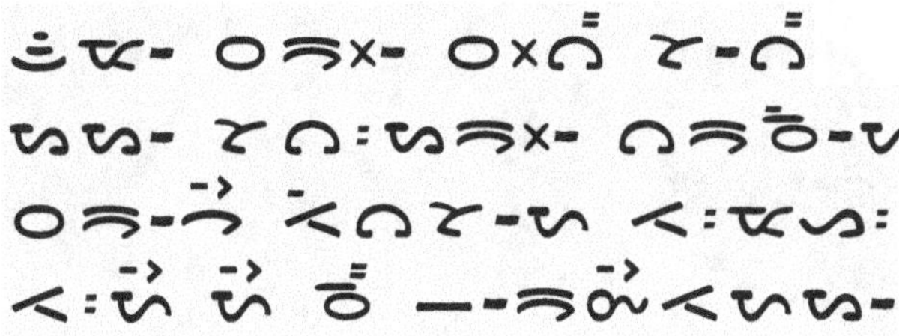

- Abugida (Insular Southeast Asian)
- Languages – Toba, Karo, Dairi, Mandailing, Simalungun, Angkola
- People – Sumatran
- Places – Sumatra (Indonesia)
- Related scripts – Brahmi, Malay
- History – circa 1300 AD to present
- Unicode block U+1BC0 – U+1BFF

# 12. Bhaiksuki (Arrow headed script)

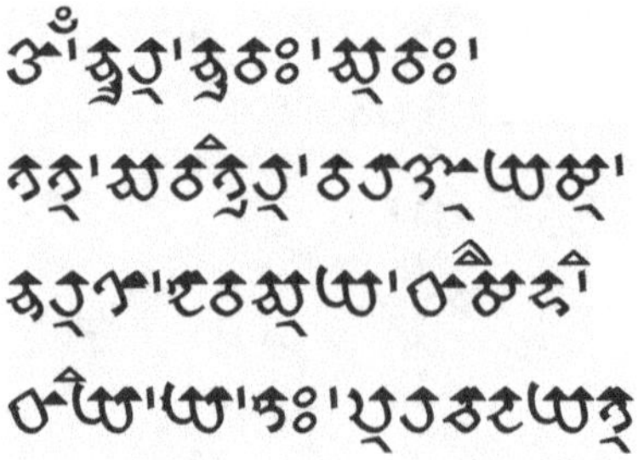

- Abugida (Indic)
- Languages – Sanskrit, Buddhist
- People – of West Bengal, Bihar
- Places – West Bengal, Bihar, Bangladesh
- Related scripts – Brahmi, Gupta, Sharada, Devanagari
- History – circa 11th – 12th century AD
- Unicode block U+11C00–U+11C6F

# 13. Brahmi (lipi)

𑀑𑀁 𑀪𑀽𑀭𑁆 𑀪𑀼𑀯𑀂 𑀲𑁆𑀯𑀂
𑀢𑀢𑁆 𑀲𑀯𑀺𑀢𑀼𑀭𑁆 𑀯𑀭𑁂𑀡𑁆𑀬𑀁
𑀪𑀭𑁆𑀕𑁄 𑀤𑁂𑀯𑀲𑁆𑀬 𑀥𑀻𑀫𑀳𑀺
𑀥𑀺𑀬𑁄 𑀬𑁄 𑀦𑀂 𑀧𑁆𑀭𑀘𑁄𑀤𑀬𑀸𑀢𑁆 ||

---

Brahmi is the forerunner of Devanagari and all Indian scripts, and also many South Asian scripts. Ancient stone inscriptions in temples & monuments are seen with this script.

- Abugida (Indic)
- Languages – Sanskrit, Pali, Prakrit, Kannada, Tamil, Buddhist
- People – Indians, South Asians, Buddhists
- Places – India, South Asia, Tibet
- Related scripts – Indus Valley, Gupta, Sharada, Devanagari, Kharosthi
- History – circa 10000 BC – 5th century AD
- Unicode block U+11000 - U+1107F
- https://en.wikipedia.org/wiki/Brahmi_script

# 14. Buginese (Lontara)

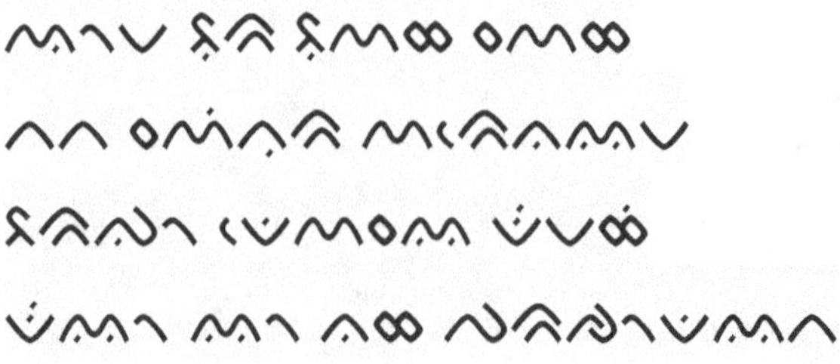

---

The Buginese script was used extensively in Indonesia before Dutch colonization.

- Abugida (Insular Southeast Asian)
- Languages – Bima, Buginese, Ende, Makassarese, Mamuju, Mandar, Sumbawa, Wotu
- People – Sulawesi
- Places – Indonesia
- Related scripts – Brahmi, Batak, Balinese
- History – circa 15th century AD to present
- Unicode block U+1A00 - U+1A1F

# 15. Buhid (Mangyan)

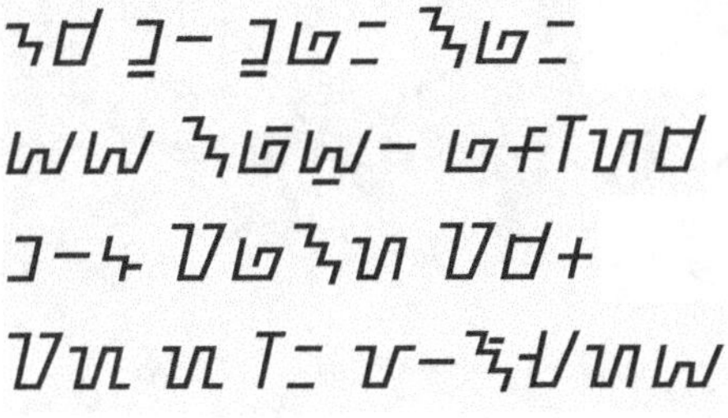

- Abugida (Insular Southeast Asian)
- Languages - Buhid, Tagalog
- People – Mangyans
- Places – Mindoro (Philippines)
- Related scripts – Brahmi, Kawi, Hanunoo, Tagbanwa
- History – circa 1300 AD to present
- Unicode block U+1740 - U+175F

# 16. Canadian Aboriginal Syllabics

ᐃᑦ ⊥ᐳr ⊥ᐳvᐊᐦ ᔆvᐊᐦ

ᗡᐪ ᙓvᐅᗞr vᐊrᐅᐣᘓᑦ

⊥ᐸrᙏ ᑐvᐊᔆᘓ dᐦīᙓᐳ

dᐳᘏ ᘏ ᓚᐦ prᐊᙏdᘓᐪ

---

- Abugida (Indigenous Canadian)
- Languages - Inuktitut, Carrier, Cree, Blackfoot, Naskapi, Ojibwe, Slavey
- People – Indigenous Canadians - Algonquian, Inuit, Athabaskan
- Places – Canada, Greenland, Alaska, Siberia, USA
- Related scripts – Devanagari, Pitman shorthand
- History – circa 1840 AD to present
- Unicode block U+1400 - U+167F, Extended U+18B0 - U+18FF, Extended A block U+11AB0 - U+11ABF

# 17. Chakma (Ojhapath)

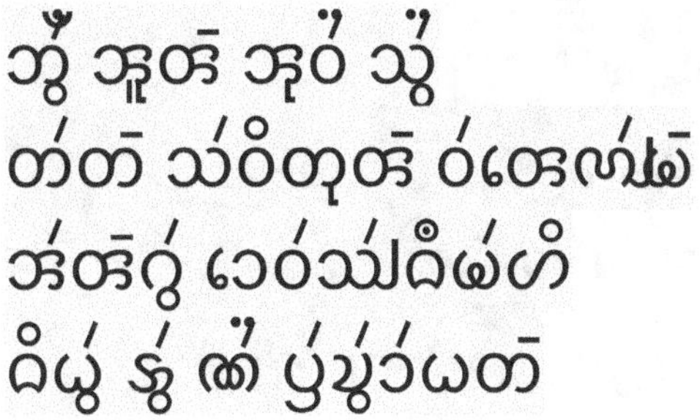

- Abugida (indic)
- Languages - Chakma, Pali, Tangchangya
- People – Chakma, Daingnet
- Places – Mizoram NE India, Bangladesh, Myanmar
- Related scripts – Brahmi, Pallava, Myanmar, Khmer
- History – circa unknown to present
- Unicode block U+11100 - U+1114F

# 18. Cham

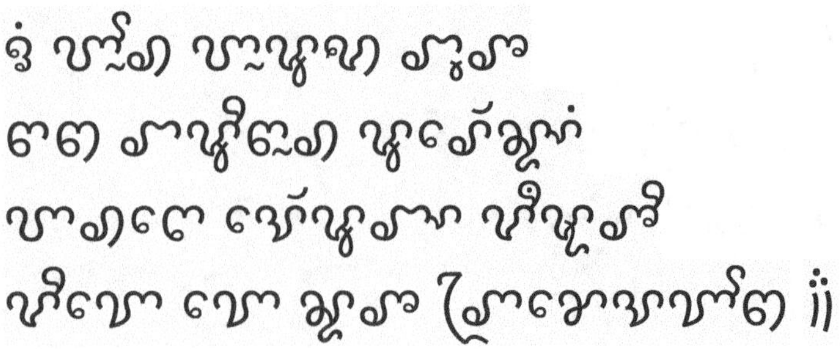

- Abugida (Mainland Southeast Asian)
- Languages - Cham, Sanskrit
- People – Cham
- Places – Vietnam, Cambodia
- Related scripts – Brahmi, Myanmar, Khmer, Grantha
- History – circa 4th century AD to present
- Unicode block U+AA00 - U+AA5F

# 19. Cherokee syllabary

ᎣᏍ Ꮹ ᏩᏮ ᎡᎠᏅ

ᏔᏔ ᏲᏫᏗ ᎥᎠᎮᏂᏬᏍ

ᎥᎠᏅᎪ ᏕᎥᎠᏪᏬ ᏧᏍᎯ

ᏧᏁ Ꮑ Ᏻ ᏯᏑᏝᏬᏔ

---

- Syllabary – (American)
- Languages – Cherokee, Iroquoian
- People – American Indian Cherokee
- Places – North and South Carolina, Tennessee, Georgia, Alabama, Oklahoma, Arkansas
- Related scripts – None
- History – circa 1820 AD to present
- Unicode block U+13A0 - U+13FF, Supplement U+AB70 - U+ABBF

## 20. Chinese characters (Han, Hanzi)

嗡 布尔 布瓦 斯瓦

**达** 萨维图尔 **瓦**伦亚姆

**巴戈 德瓦斯**亚 迪玛希

**迪**约哟 呐 [医]普拉科达亚特

---

- Logographic (East Asian)
- Languages – Chinese, Korean, Japanese
- People – Chinese
- Places – China, Taiwan, Korea, Vietnam, Japan
- Related scripts – Oracle bone script, Korean, Kanji
- History – circa 1600 BC to present
- Unicode block U+4E00 - U+9FFF

# 21. Coptic

ⲟⲙ ⲃϩⲩⲣ ⲃϩⲩⲃⲁϩ ⲥⲃⲁϩ

ⲧⲁⲧ ⲥⲁⲃⲓⲧⲩⲣ ⲃⲁⲣⲉⲛⲓⲁⲙ

ⲃϩⲁⲣⲅⲟ ⲇⲉⲃⲁⲥⲓⲁ ⲇϩⲓⲙⲁϩⲓ

ⲇϩⲓⲟ ⲓⲟ ⲛⲁϩ ⲡⲣⲁϭⲟⲇⲓⲁⲧ

---

- Alphabet (European)
- Languages – Coptic, Andaandi, Mattokki, Nobiin
- People – Copts
- Places – Egypt, Sudan
- Related scripts – Greek, Egyptian, Phoenician
- History – circa 2$^{nd}$ century AD to present
- Unicode block U+2C80 - U+2CFF, Greek and Coptic U+0370 - U+03FF, Coptic Epact Numbers U+102E0 - U+102FF

# 22. Cyrillic (Russian and Slavic)

оṃ бхӯр бхувас сваха
тат савитур варэṇйам
бхарго дэвасйа дхӣмахи
дхийо йо наха прачодайа̄т.

---

- Alphabet (European)
- Languages – Slavic
- People – Slav
- Places – Russia, Ukraine, Serbia, Tajikistan, Belarus, Bulgaria, Kazakhstan, Kyrgyzstan, North Macedonia
- Related scripts – Greek, Glagolitic, Latin
- History – circa 900 AD to present. Official Language
- Unicode block U+0400 - U+04FF, Supplement U+0500 - U+052F, Extended blocks U+2DE0 - U+2DFF, U+A640 - U+A69F, U+1C80 - U+1C8F

# 23. Dogra (Dogri, Dogra Akkhar)

𑠄𑠷 𑠡𑠰𑠤𑠹 𑠡𑠯𑠦𑠸 𑠩𑠹𑠦𑠸
𑠙𑠙𑠹 𑠩𑠦𑠭𑠙𑠯𑠤𑠹 𑠦𑠤𑠳𑠘𑠹𑠣𑠢𑠹
𑠡𑠤𑠹𑠌𑠵 𑠛𑠳𑠦𑠩𑠹𑠣 𑠜𑠮𑠢𑠪𑠭
𑠜𑠭𑠣𑠵 𑠣𑠵 𑠝𑠸 𑠞𑠹𑠤𑠏𑠵𑠛𑠣𑠬𑠙𑠹 ||

---

- Abugida (Indic)
- Languages – Dogri
- People – Dogri
- Places – Jammu, Himachal Pradesh, Punjab
- Related scripts – Brahmi, Sharada, Gurmukhi, Takri
- History – circa 1880 AD to present
- Unicode block U+11800 - U+1184F

# 24. Ethiopic (Ge'ez)

ሆም ቡር ቡው ዝውህ
ትት ዝዌቱህ ውሃኔይም
ብህጎ ዳውዝ ዴምኜ
ዴዮ ዮ ንህ ፕርቆድያት

---

- Abugida (African)
- Languages – Ethiopian, Tigre, Amharic, Tigrinya
- People – Ethiopian, Eritrean
- Places – Ethiopia, Eritrea (Africa)
- Related scripts – Proto Sinaitic, Amharic
- History – circa 1st century AD to present
- Unicode block U+1200–U+137F, Supplement U+1380–U+139F, Extended blocks U+2D80 - U+2DDF, U+AB00–U+AB2F, U+1E7E0–U+1E7FF
- https://en.wiktionary.org/wiki/Wiktionary:Ethiopic transliteration

# 25. Georgian (Mkhedruli)

ომ ბჰურ ბჰუვაჰ სვაჰ
თათ სავითურ ვარენჯამ
ბჰარგო დევასჯა დჰიმაჰი
დჰიჯო ჯო ნაჰ პრაჩოდჯათ

---

- Alphabet (European)
- Languages – Asomtavruli, Nuskhuri, Mkhedruli, Mingrelian, Svan, Laz
- People – Georgian
- Places – Georgia (East Europe), Azerbaijan, Turkey, Iran
- Related scripts – Greek
- History – circa 5th century AD to present. Official Language
- Unicode block U+ 10A0–U+10FF, Supplement U+2D00–U+2D2F, Extended U+1C90–U+1CBF

# 26. Glagolitic (Glagolitsa or Asbuka)

ⱁⰿ ⰱⱈⱆⱆⱃ ⰱⱈⱆⰲⰰⱈ ⱄⰲⰰⱈ

ⱅⰰⱅ ⱄⰰⰲⰻⱅⱆⱃ ⰲⰰⱃⰵⱀⰼⰰⰿ

ⰱⱈⰰⱃⰳⱁ ⰴⰵⰲⰰⱄⰼⰰ ⰴⱈⰻⰿⰰⱈⰻ

ⰴⱈⰻⰼⱁ ⰼⱁ ⱀⰰⱈ ⱂⱃⰰⱌⱈⱁⰴⰼⰰⱅ

---

- Alphabet (European)
- Languages – Slavonic, Chakavian, Croatian
- People – Slavic
- Places – Bulgaria, Croatia, Bohemia, Czech Republic, Slovakia, Poland, Hungary, Serbia
- Related scripts – Phoenician, Greek
- History – circa 862 to 19th century AD
- Unicode block U+2C00–U+2C5F, Supplement U+1E000–U+1E02F
- https://glagolitic.badc0de.net/

# 27. Gothic

𐍉𐌼 𐌱𐌷𐌿𐌿𐍂 𐌱𐌷𐌿𐍅𐌰𐌷 𐍃𐍅𐌰𐌷

𐍄𐌰𐍄 𐍃𐌰𐍅𐌹𐍄𐌿𐍂 𐍅𐌰𐍂𐌴𐌽𐌾𐌰𐌼

𐌱𐌷𐌰𐍂𐌲𐍉 𐌳𐌴𐍅𐌰𐍃𐌾𐌰 𐌳𐌷𐌹𐌹𐌼𐌰𐌷𐌹

𐌳𐌷𐌹𐌾𐍉 𐌾𐍉 𐌽𐌰𐌷 𐍀𐍂𐌰𐌺𐍉𐌳𐌰𐌾𐌰𐌰𐍄

---

- Alphabet (European)
- Languages – Gothic
- People – Goths
- Places – Central Europe, Scandinavia
- Related scripts – Carolingian, Greek, Runic
- History – circa 350 to 6th century AD
- Unicode block U+10330–U+1034F

# 28. Grantha

𑍐 𑌭𑍂𑌰𑍍 𑌭𑍁𑌵𑌃 𑌸𑍍𑌵𑌃
𑌤𑌤𑍍 𑌸𑌵𑌿𑌤𑍁𑌰𑍍 𑌵𑌰𑍇𑌣𑍍𑌯𑌂
𑌭𑌰𑍍𑌗𑍋 𑌦𑍇𑌵𑌸𑍍𑌯 𑌧𑍀𑌮𑌹𑌿
𑌧𑌿𑌯𑍋 𑌯𑍋 𑌨𑌃 𑌪𑍍𑌰𑌚𑍋𑌦𑌯𑌾𑌤𑍍 ॥

---

- Abugida (Indic)
- Languages – Sanskrit, Old Tamil, Tulu Malayalam
- People – South Indians
- Places – Tamil Nadu, Kerala
- Related scripts – Brahmi, Tamil, Malayalam, Khmer
- History – circa 7th century AD to present
- Unicode block U+11300–U+1137F

# 29. Greek

ομ βηορ βηοβε σβαη

τατ σαβιτορ βαρενυαμ

βηαργο δεβασυα δηιμαηι

δηιυο υο ναη πραχοδυαθ

---

- Alphabet (European)
- Languages – Greek, Albanian, Balkan, Cypriot, Turkish
- People – Greek, Cypriot
- Places – Greece, Cyprus, European Union
- Related scripts – Egyptian hieroglyphs, Phoenician, Cyrillic, Euclidean, Coptic
- History – circa 800 BC to present. Official Language
- Unicode block U+ 0370–U+03FF, Extended U+1F00–U+1FFF

## 30. Gujarati

ૐ ભૂર્ ભુવઃ સ્વઃ

તત્ સવિતુર્ વરેણ્યમ્

ભર્ગો દેવસ્ય ધીમહિ

ધિયો યો નઃ પ્રચોદયાત્ ॥

---

- Abugida (Indic)
- Languages – Gujarati, Kutchi, Chodri, Bhili, Vasavi, Avestan
- People – Gujarati, Kutchi, Zoroastrians in India
- Places – Gujarat, Kutch
- Related scripts –Brahmi, Siddham, Devanagari, Modi
- History – circa 1592 AD to present. Official Language
- Unicode block U+ 0A80–U+0AFF

# 31. Gunjala Gondi (Koytura Gunjala)

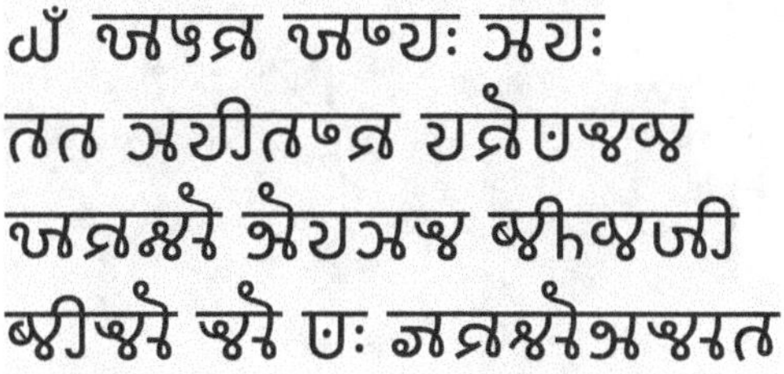

---

- Abugida (Indic)
- Languages – Gondi
- People – Gonds
- Places – Telangana, Andhra Pradesh
- Related scripts - Brahmi, Modi
- History – circa 1750 AD to present
- Unicode block U+11D60–U+11DAF

## 32. Gurmukhi (Punjabi)

ੴ ਭੂਰ੍ ਭੁਵਃ ਸ੍ਵਃ

ਤਤ੍ ਸਵਿਤੁਰ੍ ਵਰੇਣਜਮ੍

ਭਰ੍ਗੋ ਦੇਵਸਜ ਧੀਮਹਿ

ਧਿਯੋ ਯੋ ਨਃ ਪ੍ਰਚੋਦਯਾਤ੍ ॥

---

- Abugida (Indic)
- Languages – Punjabi, Saraiki, Sindhi
- People – Punjabi
- Places – Punjab, Himachal Pradesh, Kashmir, Delhi
- Related scripts - Brahmi, Sharada, Landa, Multani
- History – circa 1550 AD to present. Official Language
- Unicode block U+0A00–U+0A7F

# 33. Hanunoo

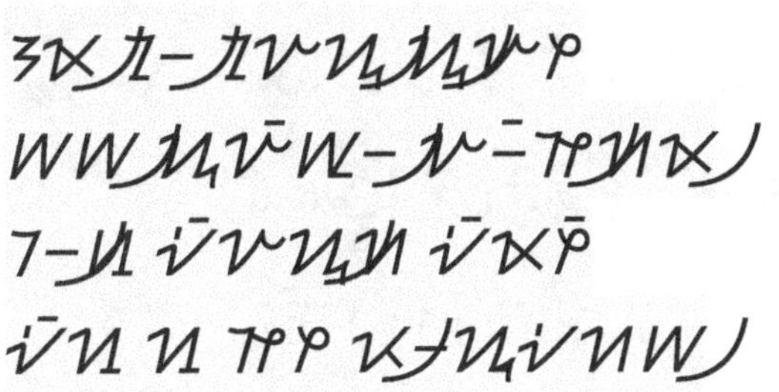

- Abugida (Southeast Asian)
- Languages – Hanunoo
- People – Mangyan
- Places – Mindoro Philippines
- Related scripts - Brahmi, Kawi, Buhid, Batak
- History – circa 1300 AD to present
- Unicode block U+1720–U+173F

# 34. Hiragana (Kiragana)

おおむ ぶうる ぶゔぁす すゔぁは

たと さゔぃとぅる ゔぁれえにゃむ

ばるごお でえゔぁすや でぃいまひ

でぃよお よお なは ぷらちょおだやあと

---

- Syllabary (East Asian)
- Languages – Japanese
- People – Japanese
- Places – Japan, Palau
- Related scripts – Oracle bone script, Kanji, Katakana
- History – circa 800 AD to present. Official Language
- Unicode block U+3040–U+309F, Kana Extended U+1AFF0–U+1AFFF, U+1B100–U+1B12F, Kana Supplement: U+1B000–U+1B0FF, Small Kana Extension: U+1B130–U+1B16F
- Also written Top-to-Bottom

# 35. Javanese (Aksara Jawa or Old Kawi)

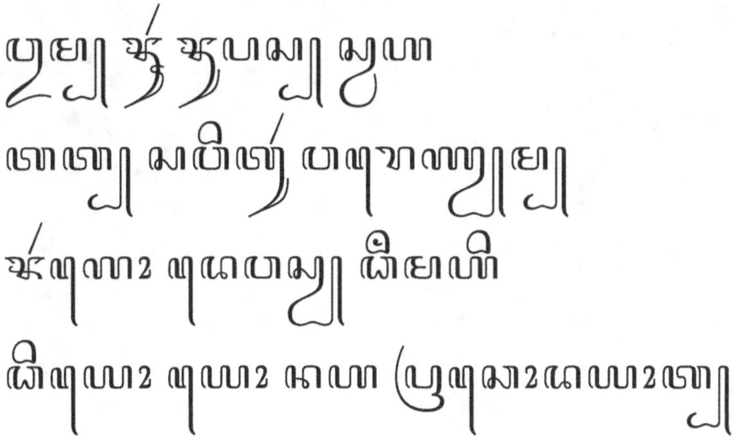

- Abugida (Insular Southeast Asian)
- Languages – Javanese, Bali, Osing, Sunda, Sanskrit, Sudanese, Madurese, Sasak, Malay
- People – Javanese
- Places – Java Indonesia, Malaysia, Singapore
- Related scripts - Brahmi, Pallava, Batak, Rejang
- History – circa 15th century AD to present
- Unicode block U+A980–U+A9DF

# 36. Kaithi (Bihar Kayastha)

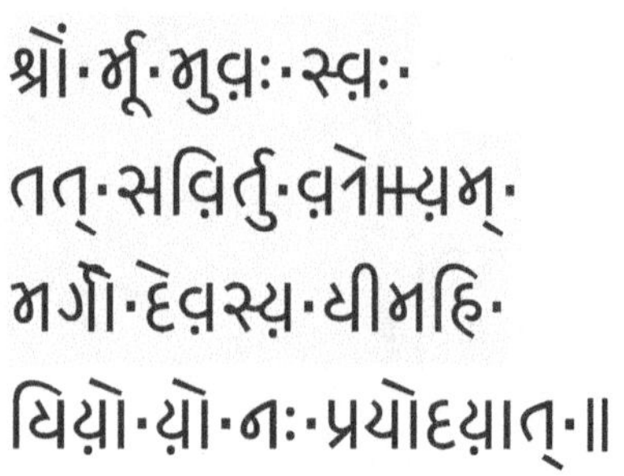

---

- Abugida (Indic)
- Languages – Bhojpuri, Magadhi, Urdu, Awadhi, Hindustani, Maithili, Bengali, Nagpuri
- People – Bihari
- Places – Bihar, Uttar Pradesh, Nepal
- Related scripts - Brahmi, Siddham, Nagari, Devanagari
- History – circa 16th century to 1950 AD
- Unicode block U+11080–U+110CF

# 37. Kannada

ಓಂ ಭೂರ್ ಭುವಃ ಸ್ವಃ

ತತ್ ಸವಿತುರ್ ವರೇಣ್ಯಮ್

ಭರ್ಗೋ ದೇವಸ್ಯ ಧೀಮಹಿ

ಧಿಯೋ ಯೋ ನಃ ಪ್ರಚೋದಯಾತ್ ||

---

- Abugida (Indic)
- Languages – Kannada, Konkani, Tulu, Paniya, Sanskrit
- People – Kannadiga, Dravidian
- Places – Karnataka
- Related scripts - Brahmi, Kadamba, Telugu
- History – circa 1300 AD to present. Official Language
- Unicode block U+0C80–U+0CFF

# 38. Katakana

オーム ブール ブヴァス スヴァハ
タト サヴィトゥル ヴァレーニャム
バルゴー デーヴァスヤ ディーマヒ
ディヨー ヨーナハ プラチョーダヤート

---

- Syllabary (East Asian)
- Languages – Japanese, Ryukyuan, Ainu, Central Okinawan, Taiwanese Hokkien
- People – Japanese
- Places – Japan, Palau
- Related scripts – Oracle bone script, Kanji, Hiragana
- History – circa 800 AD to present. Official Language
- Unicode block U+30A0–U+30FF, Katakana Phonetic Extensions U+31F0-U+31FF, Kana Extended U+1AFF0–U+1AFFF, U+1B100–U+1B12F, Kana Supplement: U+1B000–U+1B0FF, Small Kana Extension: U+1B130–U+1B16F
- Also written Top-to-Bottom

# 39. Kayah Li

ꤢ꤭ꤝ ꤊꤛꤢꤨꤔ ꤊꤛꤢꤨꤗꤢꤛ ꤞꤗꤢꤛ
ꤟꤢꤟ ꤞꤢꤗꤓꤟꤢꤨꤔ ꤗꤢꤔꤢꤧꤒꤢꤝ
ꤊꤛꤢꤔꤠꤢ꤭ ꤐꤢꤧꤗꤢꤞꤙꤢ ꤐꤛꤓꤝꤢꤛꤓ
ꤐꤛꤓꤙꤢ꤭ ꤙꤢ꤭ ꤘꤢꤛ ꤕꤔꤢꤚꤢ꤭ꤐꤢꤙꤢꤟ

---

- Alphabet (Mainland Southeast Asian)
- Languages – Kayah, Karen
- People – Burmese
- Places – Burma, Thailand
- Related scripts - Brahmi, Myanmar
- History – circa 1962 AD to present
- Unicode block U+A900–U+A92F

# 40. Kharoshthi

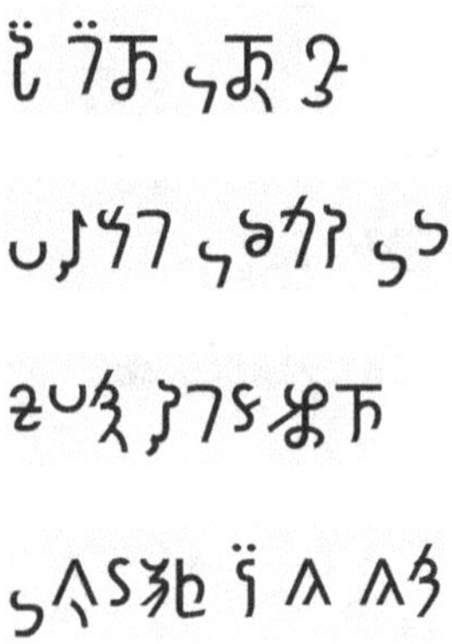

- Abugida (Indic)
- Languages – Prakrit, Gandhari, Pali, Saka
- People – Indian, Central Asian
- Places – Northern Pakistan, Eastern Afghanistan, Bacteria, Uzbekistan
- Related scripts – Indus, Brahmi, Aramaic
- History – circa 4th century BC to 3rd century AD
- Unicode block U+10A00–U+10A5F

# 41. Khmer

ឱម៑ ភូរ៑ ភុវស៑ ស្វហ
តត៑ សវិតុរ៑ វរេណ្យម៑
ភគ៌ោ ទេវស្យ ធីមហិ
ធិយោ យោ នហ ប្រចោទយាត៑

---

- Abugida (Mainland Southeast Asian)
- Languages – Khmer, Brao, Jarai, Kavet, Tampuan, Pali, Sanskrit
- People – Cambodian
- Places – Cambodia, Laos, Thailand
- Related scripts – Pallava, Khom Thai, Grantha
- History – circa 611 AD to present. Official Language
- Unicode block U+1780–U+17FF, Khmer Symbols U+19E0–U+19FF

# 42. Khojki

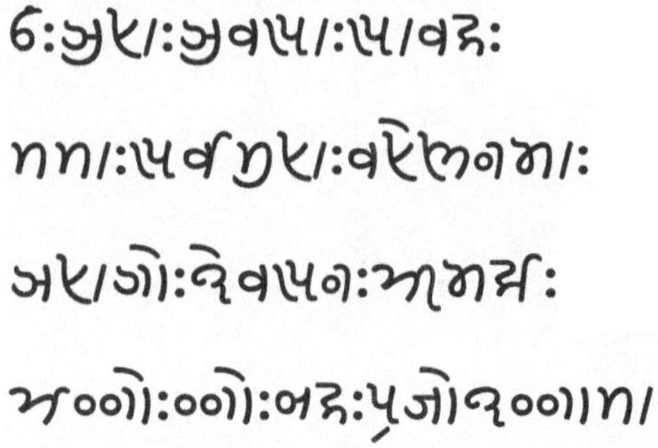

- Abugida (Indic)
- Languages – Kutchi Gujarati, Sindhi, Punjabi
- People – Khoja, Sindhi
- Places – India, Pakistan, East Africa
- Related scripts – Sharada, Landa, Gurmukhi
- History – circa 14th century AD to present
- Unicode block U+11200–U+1124F

# 43. Khom Thai (Akson Khom)

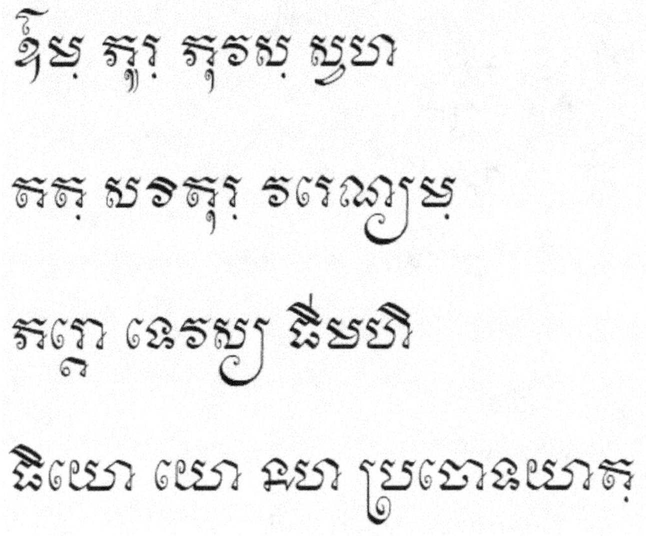

---

- Abugida (Indic)
- Languages – Pali, Sanskrit, Khmer, Thai
- People – Thai, Lao
- Places – Thailand, Laos
- Related scripts – Brahmi, Pallava, Sukhothai
- History – circa 1400 AD to present
- Unicode block NONE
- http://skyknowledge.com/orthographies.htm

# 44. Khudawadi (Sindhi)

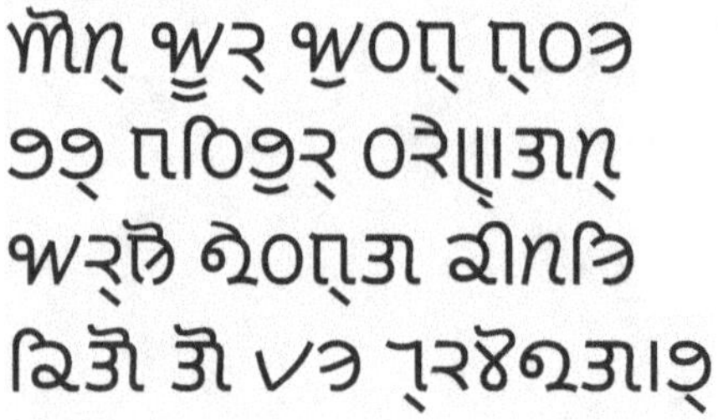

- Abugida (Indic)
- Languages – Sindhi
- People – Sindhi
- Places – Sindh India, Sindh Pakistan
- Related scripts – Sharada, Landa, Gurmukhi, Multani
- History – circa 16th century AD to present
- Unicode block U+ 112B0–U+112FF

# 45. Korean (Hangul, Choson'gul)

옴 부르 부바 스바

타트 사비 투르 바레 얌

바르고 데바 시아 디마히

디오 요 나 프라 쵸다 야트

---

- Syllabary (East Asian)
- Languages – Korean, Jeju, Taiwanese, Cia Cia
- People – Korean, Jilin Chinese
- Places – South Korea, North Korea, Taiwan, China, Indonesia
- Related scripts – Idu, Gukyeol, Hanja
- History – circa 1443 AD to present. Official Language
- Unicode block U+1100–U+11FF, U+3130–U+318F, U+A960–U+A97F, U+D7B0–U+D7FF
- https://translate.yandex.com/?lang=la-ko
- https://en.wikipedia.org/wiki/McCune%E2%80%93Reischauer

# 46. Lao (Akson Lao)

ໂອມ ພູຣ ພຸວັສ ສວະຫະ
ຕັຕ ສະວິຕຸຣ ວະເຣນຍັມ
ພັຣໂຄ ເທວັສຍະ ທີມະຫີ
ທີໂຍ ໂຍ ນະຫະ ປຣະໂຈທະຍາຕ

---

- Abugida (Mainland Southeast Asian)
- Languages – Lao, Bruo, Jeh, Kuay, Tai Dam, Isan, Thai
- People – Lao, Thai
- Places – Laos, Thailand
- Related scripts – Brahmi, Pallava, Thai
- History – circa 1350 AD to present. Official Language
- Unicode block U+ 0E80–U+0EFF

# 47. Lepcha (Rong)

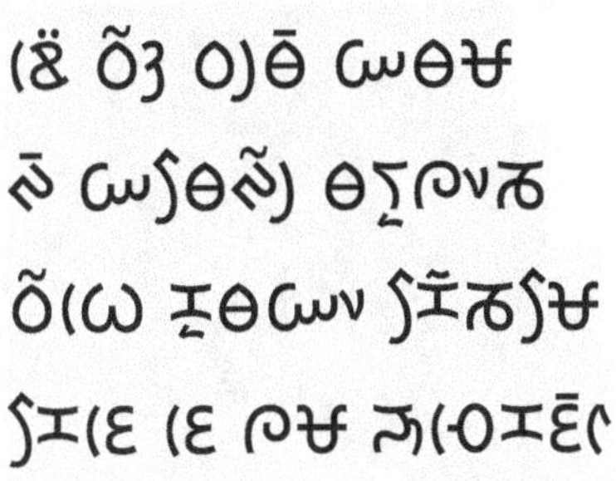

- Abugida (Central Asian)
- Languages – Lepcha, Tibeto Burman
- People – Rong
- Places – Sikkim, Nepal, Bhutan
- Related scripts – Brahmi, Tibetan, Limbu, Phags-pa
- History – circa 1700 AD to present
- Unicode block U+1C00–U+1C4F

# 48. Limbu (Kiranti)

[illegible]
[illegible]
[illegible]
[illegible]

---

- Abugida (Indic)
- Languages – Limbu, Sino-Tibetan
- People – Limbu
- Places – Nepal, bordering India, Central Himalayas
- Related scripts – Brahmi, Tibetan, Lepcha
- History – circa 1740 AD to present
- Unicode block U+1900–U+194F

# 49. Lycian

𐊀𐊒𐊎 𐊂𐊁𐊒𐊕 𐊂𐊁𐊒𐊇𐊀𐊁 𐊖𐊇𐊀𐊁
𐊗𐊀𐊗 𐊖𐊀𐊇𐊛𐊗𐊒𐊕 𐊇𐊀𐊕𐊊𐊏𐊛𐊆𐊀𐊎
𐊂𐊁𐊀𐊕𐊄𐊒 𐊅𐊊𐊇𐊀𐊖𐊆𐊀 𐊅𐊁𐊛𐊎𐊀𐊁𐊛
𐊅𐊁𐊛𐊆𐊒 𐊆𐊒 𐊏𐊀𐊁 𐊓𐊕𐊀𐊋𐊒𐊅𐊆𐊀𐊗

---

- Alphabet (European)
- Languages – Lycian
- People – Lycian
- Places – Lycia Turkey
- Related scripts – Greek, Lydian, Phrygian
- History – circa 500 BC to 330 BC
- Unicode block U+10280–U+1029F

## 50. Mahajani

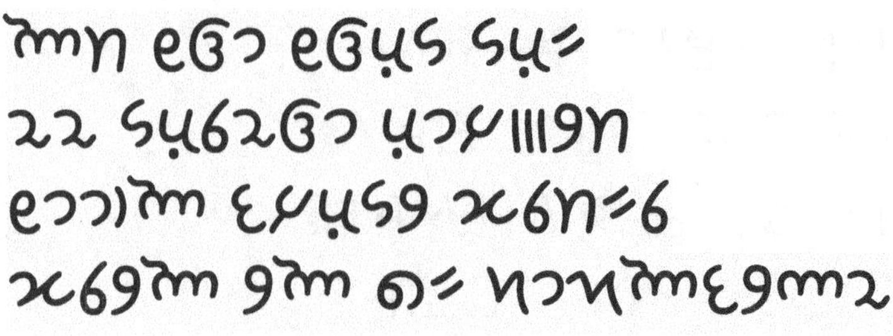

- Alphabet (Indic)
- Languages – Hindi, Punjabi, Marwari
- People – Mahajans
- Places – North India, Pakistan
- Related scripts – Sharada, Landa, Gurmukhi, Multani
- History – circa 16th century AD to present
- Unicode block U+11150–U+1117F

# 51. Malayalam

ഓം ഭൂര്ഭുവഃ സ്വഃ
തത്സവിതുര്വരേണ്യം
ഭര്ഗോ ദേവസ്യ ധീമഹി
ധിയോ യോ നഃ പ്രചോദയാത്

---

- Abugida (Indic)
- Languages – Malayalam, Sanskrit, Tulu, Konkani, Paniya
- People – Malayali, Dravidian
- Places – Kerala, Puducherry, Lakshadweep
- Related scripts – Brahmi, Grantha, Saurashtra
- History – circa 830 AD to present. Official Language
- Unicode block U+0D00–U+0D7F

# 52. Marchen (Greater Mar)

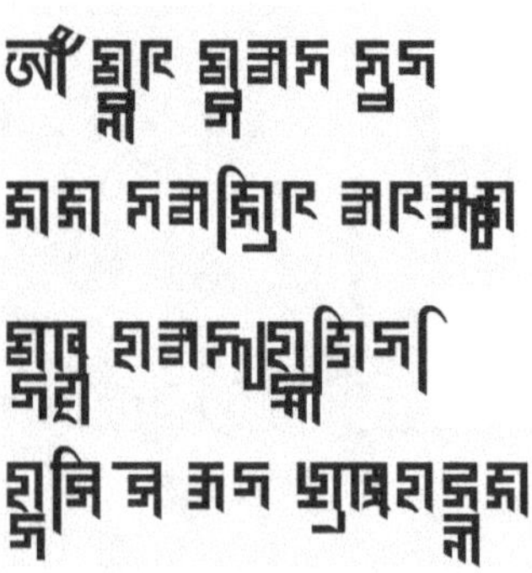

- Abugida (Indic)
- Languages – Tibetan Bon, Zhang zhung, Tibetan
- People – Tibetan Bon
- Places – Tibet
- Related scripts – Brahmi, Tibetan, Phags-pa, Lepcha
- History – circa 7th to 10th century AD
- Unicode block U+11C70–U+11CBF

# 53. Meetei Mayek (Manipuri)

[illegible]
[illegible]
[illegible]
[illegible] ॥

---

- Abugida (Indic)
- Languages – Meitei, Old Manipuri
- People – Meitei
- Places – Manipur
- Related scripts – Brahmi, Tibetan, Phags-pa, Lepcha
- History – circa 1100 AD to present
- Unicode block U+ABC0–U+ABFF Meetei Mayek Extensions U+AAE0–U+AAFF

# 54. Modi (Mudiya)

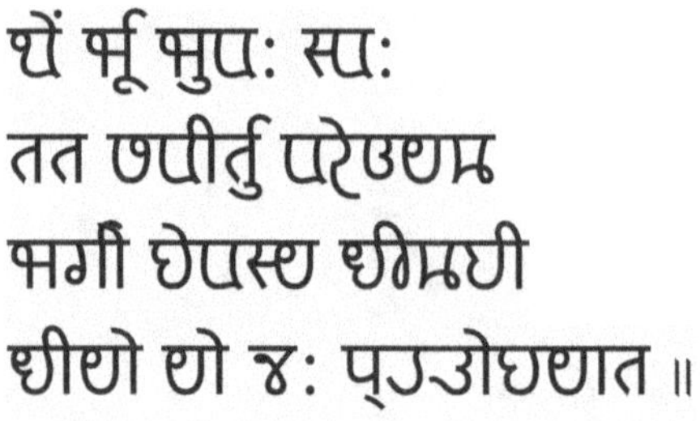

---

- Abugida (Indic)
- Languages – Marathi, Konkani, Hindi, Gujarati, Sanskrit, Kannada
- People – Maharashtrian
- Places – Maharashtra
- Related scripts – Brahmi, Siddham, Kaithi, Devanagari
- History – circa 17th century to 1950
- Unicode block U+11600–U+1165F

## 55. Mro (Mru)

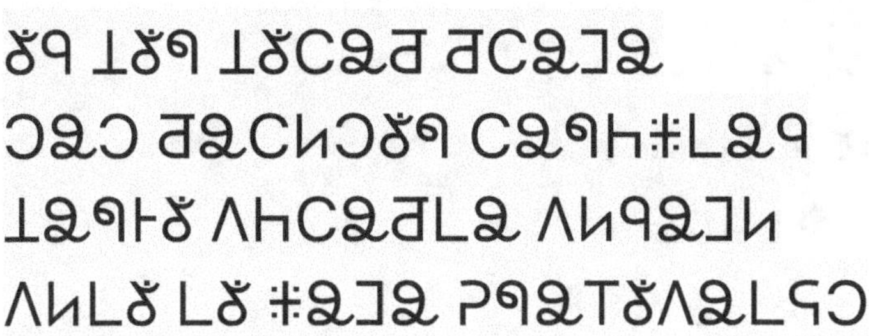

- Abugida (Indic)
- Languages – Marathi, Konkani, Hindi, Gujarati, Sanskrit, Kannada
- People – Mrus
- Places – Bangladesh, Burma, India
- Related scripts – Sino Tibetan
- History – circa 1980 to present
- Unicode block U+16A40 - U+16A6F

# 56. Multani (Sarai)

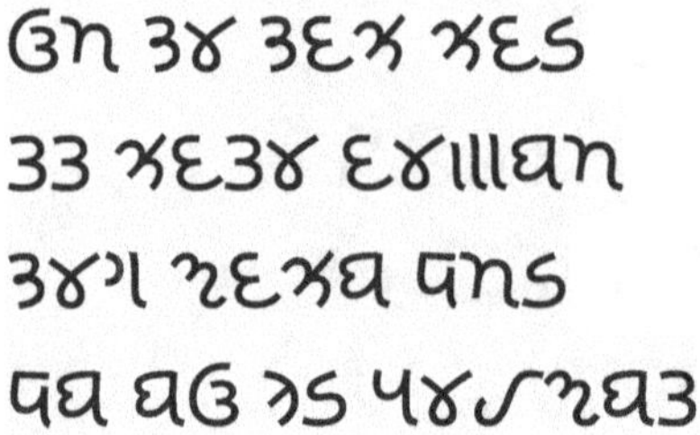

- Abjad (Indic)
- Languages – Saraiki
- People – Multani
- Places – Multan India, Sindh Pakistan
- Related scripts – Brahmi, Sharada, Landa, Mahajani
- History – circa 18th to 20th century AD
- Unicode block U+11280–U+112AF

# 57. Myanmar (Burmese/Khamti Shan)

ဥုံ ဘူရ် ဘုဝး သွး
တတ် သဝိတုရ် ဝရေဏျမ်
ဘဂေါ် ဒေဝသျ ဓိမဟိ
ဓိယော ယော နး ပြစောဒယာတ်

---

- Abugida (Mainland Southeast Asian)
- Languages – Burmese, Mon, Karen, Pali, Sanskrit
- People – Burmese
- Places – Myanmar (Burma), Thailand
- Related scripts – Brahmi, Pallava, Chakma, Shan
- History – circa 11th century AD to present
- Unicode block U+1000–U+109F, Myanmar Extended U+AA60–U+AA7F, U+A9E0–U+A9FF

# 58. Nandinagari

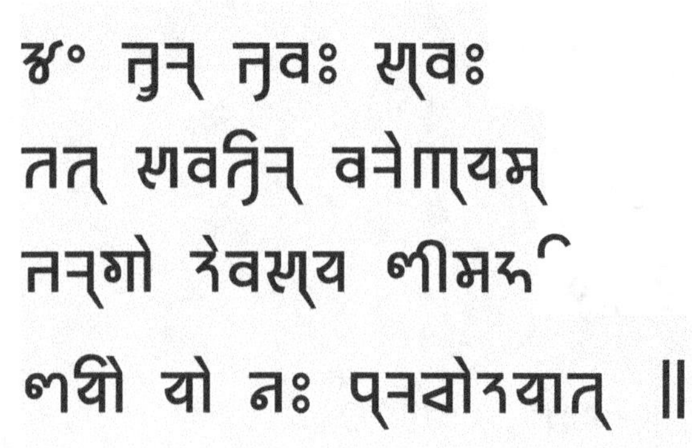

- Abugida (Indic)
- Languages – Sanskrit, Kannada
- People – Kannadiga
- Places – Karnataka, South India
- Related scripts – Brahmi, Siddham, Devanagari
- History – circa $8^{th}$ to $19^{th}$ century AD
- Unicode block U+119A0–U+119FF

# 59. New Tai Lue (Xishuangbanna Dai)

ᦵᦙᧁ ᦔᦲᦳᧉ ᦔᦲᦳᦢᧉ ᦈᧉ
ᦎᦎ ᦉᦢᦂᦎᦳᧉ ᦄᦂᦍᦙᧁ
ᦔᧉᦲᦷ ᦃᦂᦢᦵᦷᦰ ᦃᦂᦙᦳᦂ
ᦃᦂᦰᦵ ᦰᦵ ᦙᦷᧉ ᦗᦷᦎᦵᦃᦍᦱᦶ

---

- Abugida (Mainland Southeast Asian)
- Languages – Tai Lu
- People – Chinese
- Places – Jinghong China, Burma, Lao, Thailand Vietnam
- Related scripts – Brahmi, Lanna, Burmese, Tai Tham
- History – circa 1950 AD to present
- Unicode block U+1980–U+19DF

# 60. Newa (Prachalit/Nepal Bhasa/Newar)

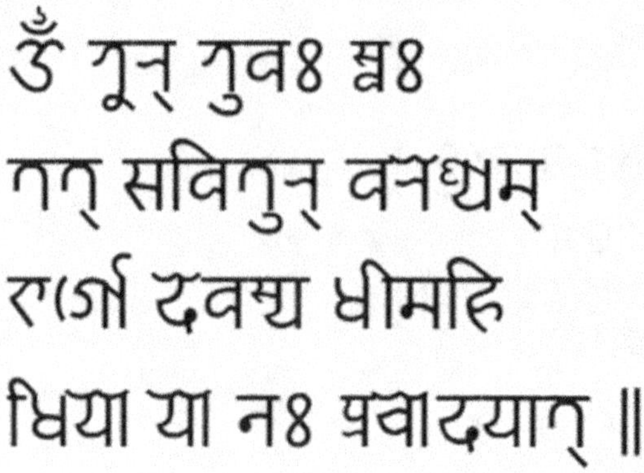

---

- Abugida (Indic)
- Languages – Nepal Bhasa, Sanskrit, Pali, Hindi, Bengali
- People – Nepali
- Places – Nepal, Sikkim India, Tibet
- Related scripts – Brahmi, Siddham, Devanagari, Ranjana
- History – circa $10^{th}$ century AD to present
- Unicode block U+11400 - U+1147F

Note:
Nepal Bhasa *language* is different from Nepali *language*. The Newa script is used to write Nepal Bhasa whereas Devanagari script is used to write Nepali.

# 61. Ol Chiki (Ol Chemet or Santali)

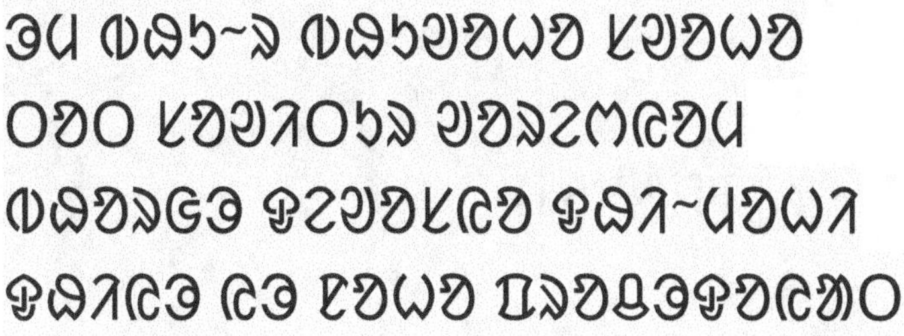

- Alphabet (Indic)
- Languages – Santali
- People – Santal
- Places – Jharkhand, Bihar, West Bengal, Orissa, Bangladesh, Nepal, Bhutan
- Related scripts – Latin
- History – circa 1925 AD to present
- Unicode block U+1C50 - U+1C7F

# 62. Old Italic (Etruscan)

OΓ BBYP BBYFAB ⟩FAB

TAT ⟩AFITYP FAPEΓyAΓ

BBAPgO DEFA⟩yA DBIΓAB I

DBIyO yO ΓAB ΓPA(BODAyAT

---

- Alphabet (European)
- Languages – Etruscan, Oscan, Paelignian, Venetic
- People – Italian
- Places – Italy
- Related scripts – Phoenician, Greek, Latin
- History – circa 700 BC to 100 BC
- Unicode block U+10300–U+1032F
- https://lingojam.com/OldItalicAlphabet

# 63. Old Permic (Abur)

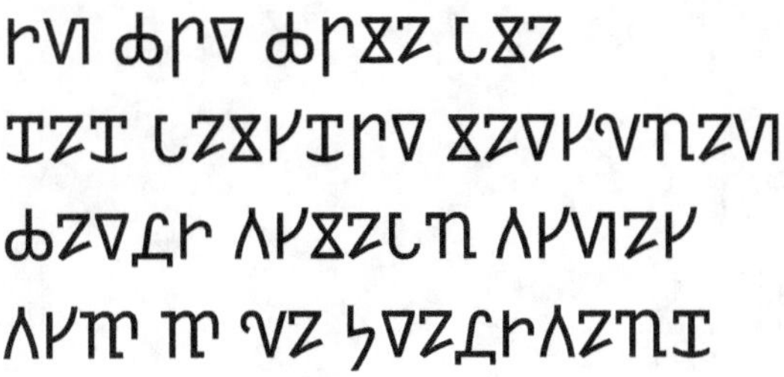

- Alphabet (European), Languages – Komi
- People – Russian, Places – Russia
- Related scripts – Phoenician, Greek, Cyrillic
- History – circa 1372 to 17th century AD
- Unicode block U+10350–U+1037F

# 64. Old Persian cuneiform

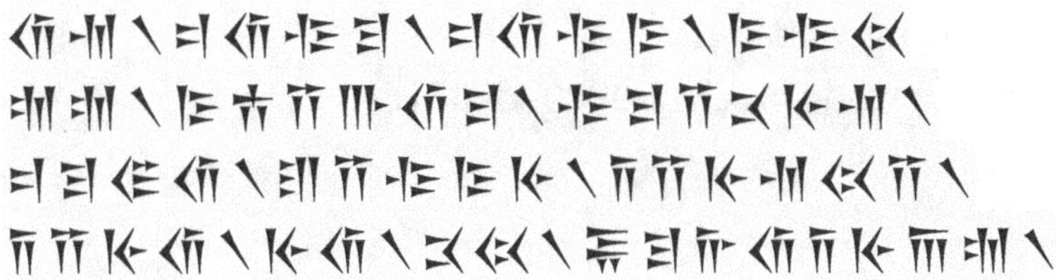

- Cuneiform (Middle Eastern), Languages – Old Persian, Babylonian
- People – Persians, Places – Iran, Turkey
- Related scripts – None
- History – circa 525 BC to 330 BC
- Unicode block U+103A0–U+103D5

# 65. Oriya (Odia)

ଓଁ ଭୂର୍ ଭୁବଃ ସ୍ୱଃ
ତତ୍ ସବିତୁର୍ ବରେଣ୍ୟମ୍
ଭର୍ଗୋ ଦେବସ୍ୟ ଧୀମହି
ଧିୟୋ ଯୋ ନଃ ପ୍ରଚୋଦୟାତ୍ ॥

---

- Abugida (Indic)
- Languages – Odia, Sanskrit, Koya, Munda, Santali
- People – Odia
- Places – Odisha (Orissa), West Bengal, Jharkhand
- Related scripts – Brahmi, Siddham, Bengali, Kalinga
- History – circa 14th century AD to present. Official Language
- Unicode block U+0B00–U+0B7F

# 66. Osage

Oᴦ Ꝛ ꞦUϟλᒍ Çϟλᒍ
ƊλƊ Çλϟ∩ƊUᒍ ϟλᒍΛᒐ∩λᴦ
ꞦϦO ƊΛϟλÇ∩λ Ɗᒍ∩ᴦλᒍ∩
ƊᒍO ᒍO ᒐλᒍ ꞦƧᒍOƊλ∩λƊ

---

- Alphabet (American)
- Languages – Osage
- People – Osage native American Indian
- Places – Oklahoma USA
- Related scripts – Greek, Latin
- History – circa 2006 AD to present
- Unicode block U+104B0–U+104FF

# 67. Ranjana (Lantsa, Nepali Calligraphic)

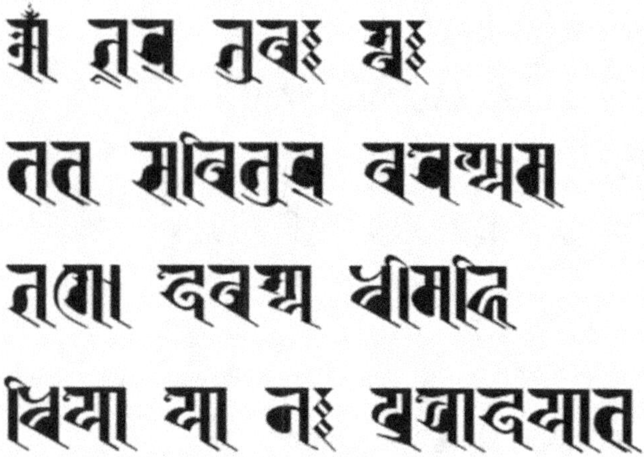

- Abugida (Indic)
- Languages – Nepal Bhasa (Newar), Sanskrit, Tibetan
- People – Newar
- Places – Nepal, Buddhist Monasteries elsewhere
- Related scripts – Brahmi, Siddham, Prachalit
- History – circa 1100 AD to present. Official
- Unicode block U+11500–U+1157F

# 68. Rejang (Redjang or Kaganga)

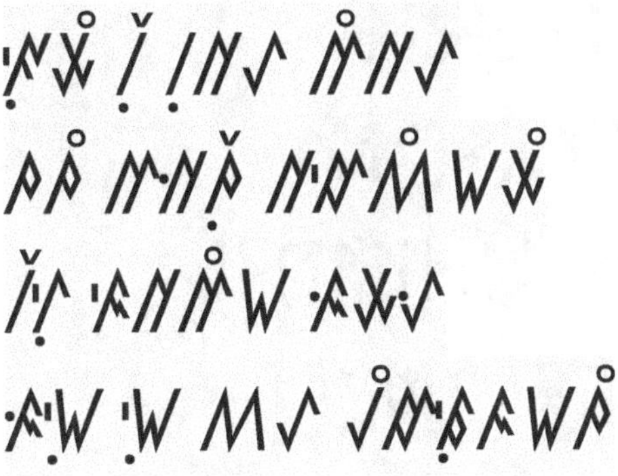

- Abugida (Insular Southeast Asian)
- Languages – Rejang, Kerinci, Lampung Api, Malay
- People – Sumatran
- Places – Sumatra Indonesia
- Related scripts – Brahmi, Pallava, Javanese
- History – circa 18th century to present
- Unicode block U+A930–U+A95F

## 69. Runic (Futhark/Gothenburg)

ᚲᛗ ᛒᚺᚼᛒᚺᚢᚹᚨᚺ ᛊᚹᚨᚺ

ᛏᚨᛏ ᛊᚨᚹᛁᛏᚢᛉ ᚹᚨᛉᛦᚾᛁᛃᚨᛗ

ᛒᚺᚨᛉᚷᚲ ᛞᛁᚹᚨᛊᛃᚨ ᛞᚺᛁᛗᚨᚺᛁ

ᛞᚺᛁᛃᚲ ᛃᚲ ᚾᚨᚺ ᛈᛉᚨᚲᚲᛞᛃᚨᛏ

---

- Alphabet (European)
- Languages – Old Norse, Germanic
- People – Germanic
- Places – Central Europe, Britain, Scandinavia
- Related scripts – Phoenician, Greek, Old Italic
- History – circa 150 to 1100 AD, also till 20th century
- Unicode block U+16A0–U+16FF

# 70. Saurashtra

ꢏꢀ ꢩꢹꢬ꣄ ꢩꢸꢮꢁ ꢱ꣄ꢮꢁ
ꢡꢡ꣄ ꢱꢮꢶꢡꢸꢬ꣄ ꢮꢬꢾꢠ꣄ꢫꢪ꣄
ꢩꢬ꣄ꢔꢵ ꢣꢾꢮꢱ꣄ꢫ ꢤꢷꢪꢲꢶ
ꢤꢶꢫꢵ ꢫꢵ ꢥꢁ ꢦ꣄ꢬꢗꢵꢣꢫꢵꢡ꣄ ॥

---

- Abugida (Indic)
- Languages – Saurashtra
- People – Saurashtrians (who migrated from Gujarat to Tamil Nadu)
- Places – Tamil Nadu, South India
- Related scripts – Brahmi, Pallava, Grantha
- History – circa 19th century AD to present
- Unicode block U+A880–U+A8DF

# 71. Sharada

𑇄 𑆨𑆷𑆫𑇀 𑆨𑆶𑆮𑆂 𑆱𑇀𑆮𑆂

𑆠𑆠𑇀 𑆱𑆮𑆴𑆠𑆶𑆫𑇀 𑆮𑆫𑆼𑆟𑇀𑆪𑆁

𑆨𑆫𑇀𑆓𑆾 𑆢𑆼𑆮𑆱𑇀𑆪 𑆣𑆵𑆩𑆲𑆴

𑆣𑆴𑆪𑆾 𑆪𑆾 𑆤𑆂 𑆥𑇀𑆫𑆖𑆾𑆢𑆪𑆳𑆠𑇀 ॥

---

- Abugida (Indic)
- Languages – Sanskrit, Kashmiri
- People – Kashmiri
- Places – Kashmir, Punjab, Pakistan, Central Asia
- Related scripts – Brahmi, Gupta, Siddham, Tibetan
- History – circa 200 to 1300 AD. Being revived
- Unicode block U+11180–U+111DF
- https://sourceforge.net/projects/advaita-sharada-font/
- https://www.amazon.com/dp/8194600812/

## 72. Siddham (Siddhamatrika, bonji)

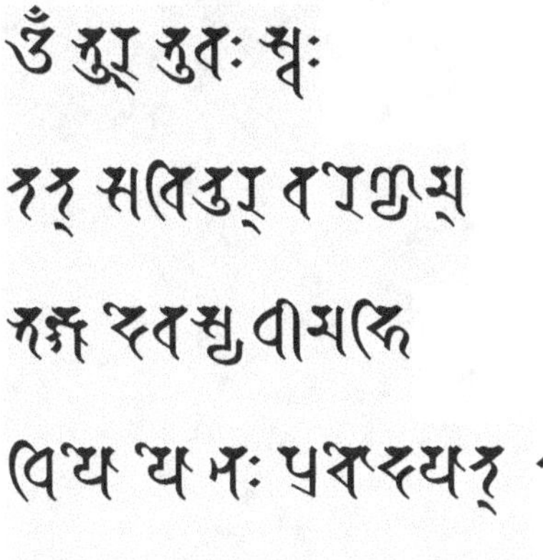

- Abugida (Indic), Languages – Sanskrit, Buddhist
- People – Indian, Buddhist
- Places – India, Japan, China, Korea, Central Asia
- Related scripts – Brahmi, Gupta, Sharada, Tibetan
- History – circa 6th century to 1200 AD
- Unicode block U+11580–U+115FF

## 73. Sinhala

ඕං භූර් භුවඃ ස්වඃ
තත් සවිතුර් වරේණ්‍යම්
භර්ගෝ දේවස්‍ය ධීමහි
ධියෝ යෝ නඃ ප්‍රචෝදයාත්

- Abugida (Indic), Languages – Sinhala, Sanskrit, Pali
- People – Sri Lankan, Places – Sri Lanka
- Related scripts – Brahmi, Grantha
- History – circa 300 AD to present. Official Language
- Unicode block U+0D80–U+0DFF, 111E0-111FF

## 74. Sora Sompeng

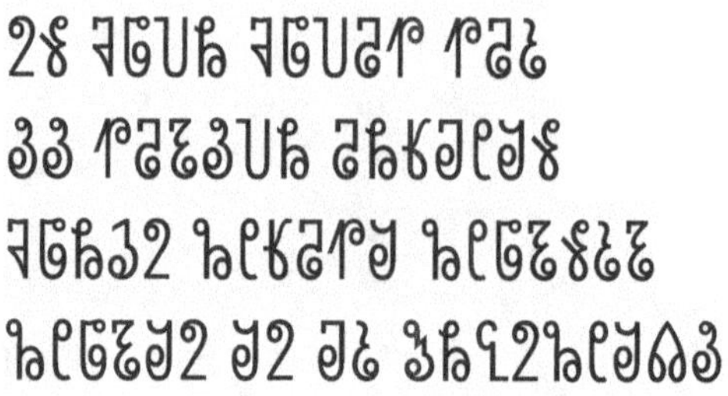

---

- Syllabary (Indic), Languages – Sora
- People – Munda, Places – Odisha India
- Related scripts – NONE
- History – circa 1936 AD to present
- Unicode block U+110D0–U+110FF

## 75. Soyombo

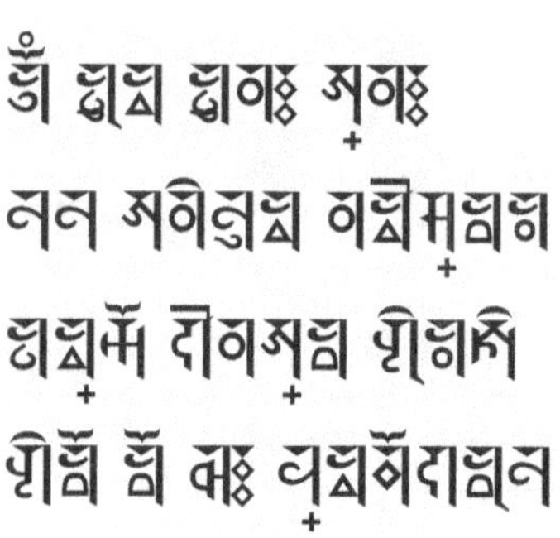

---

- Abugida (Indic), Languages – Mongolian, Tibetan, Sanskrit, People – Mongolian, Places –Mongolia
- Related scripts – Brahmi, Siddham, Devanagari
- History – circa 1686 to 18$^{th}$ century AD
- Unicode block U+11A50–U+11AAF

## 76. Sudanese (Aksara Sunda Baku)

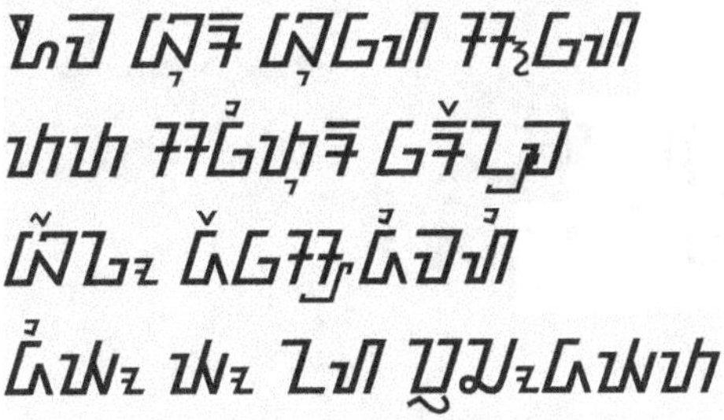

- Abugida (Insular SE Asian), Languages – Sudanese
- People – Java, Places – Java Indonesia
- Related scripts – Brahmi, Pallava, Javanese
- History – circa 1996 AD to present. Official Language
- Unicode block U+1B80–U+1BBF, 1CC0-1CCF

## 77. Sylheti Nagri (Syloti Nagri)

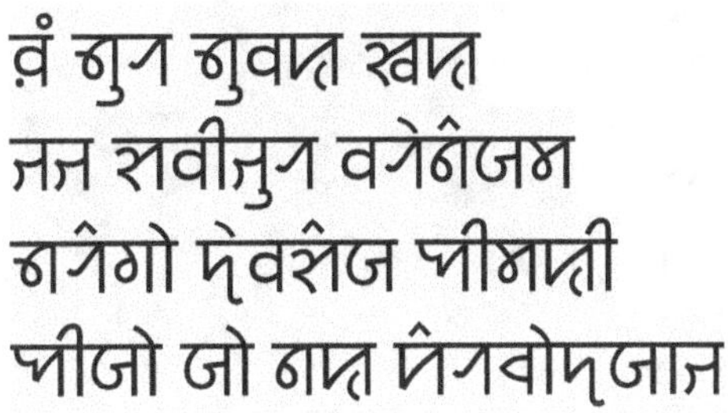

- Abugida (Indic), Languages – Sylheti, Bengali, Noakhailla,
- People – Java, Places – Bengal, Assam, Tripura
- Related scripts – Brahmi, Siddham, Kaithi
- History – circa 16th century AD to present
- Unicode block U+A800–U+A82F

## 78. Tagalog (Baybayin)

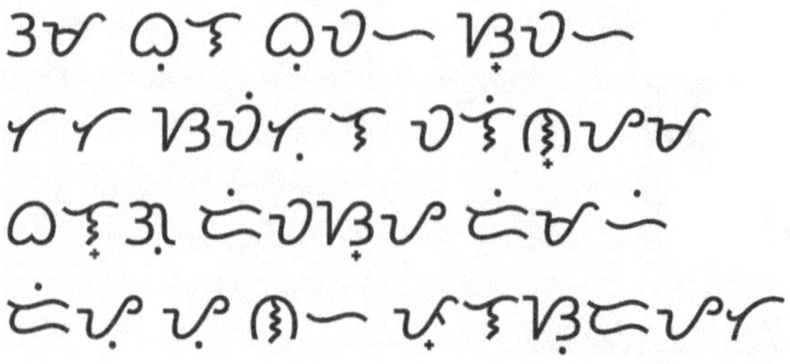

- Abugida (Insular SE Asian), Languages – Tagalog, Filipino, Ilocano,
- People – Filipino, Places – Philippines
- Related scripts –Brahmi, Pallava, Kawi, Buhid, Batak
- History – circa 13th to 18th century AD
- Unicode block U+1700–U+171F

## 79. Tagbanwa (Apurahuano)

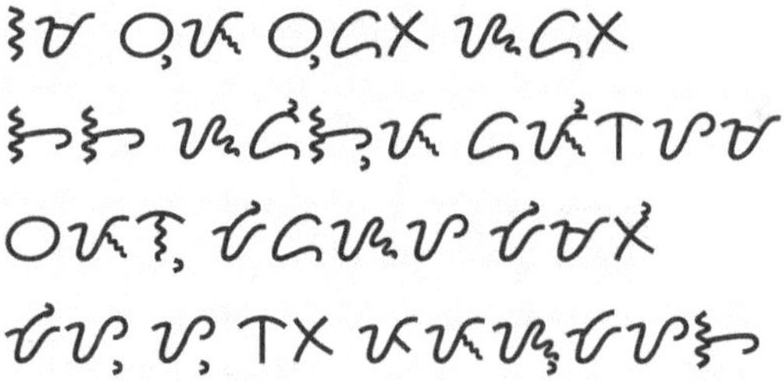

- Abugida (Insular SE Asian), Languages – Tagbanwa
- People – Tagbanwa, Palawan, Places – Philippines
- Related scripts –Brahmi, Pallava, Tagalog, Buhid
- History – circa 1300 AD to present
- Unicode block U+1760–U+177F

# 80. Tai Viet

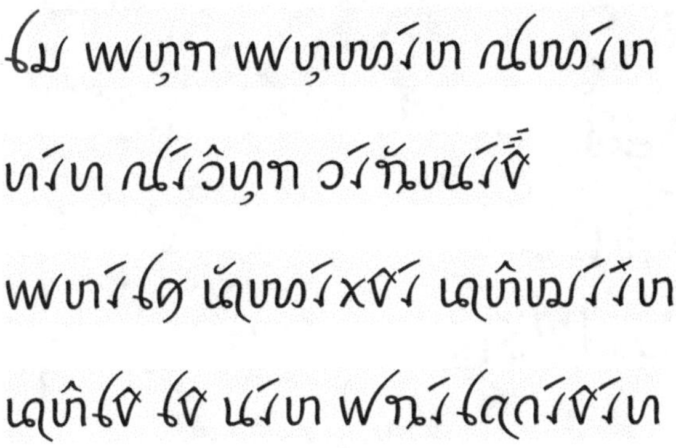

---

- Abugida (Mainland Southeast Asian)
- Languages – Tai Dam, Tai Don, Tai Daeng, Thai Song, Tay Tac
- People – Vietnamese
- Places – Vietnam, Laos, Thailand, China
- Related scripts – Brahmi, Pallava, Khmer, Thai
- History – circa 16[th] century AD to present
- Unicode block U+AA80–U+AADF

# 81. Takri (Tankri)

𑚈𑚫 𑚡𑚱𑚤𑚶 𑚡𑚰𑚦𑚬 𑚨𑚶𑚦𑚬
𑚙𑚙𑚶 𑚨𑚦𑚮𑚙𑚰𑚤𑚶 𑚦𑚤𑚲𑚘𑚶𑚣𑚫
𑚡𑚤𑚶𑚌𑚴 𑚛𑚲𑚦𑚨𑚶𑚣 𑚜𑚯𑚢𑚩𑚮
𑚜𑚮𑚣𑚴 𑚣𑚴 𑚝𑚬 𑚞𑚶𑚤𑚏𑚴𑚛𑚣𑚭𑚙𑚶 ॥

---

- Abugida (Indic)
- Languages – Chambeali, Dogri, Pahari, Kangri
- People – North Indian
- Places – Jammu & Kashmir, Punjab, Himachal Pradesh, Uttarakhand
- Related scripts – Brahmi, Gupta, Sharada, Landa
- History – circa 16th century AD to present
- Unicode block U+11680–U+116CF

## **82.** Tamil

ஓம் புபூர்வ சிவ
தட்டசைவிட்டுருவாரென்யா
பர்கோ தேவஸ்ய தீமஹி
டியோ யோ ந ப்ரச்சோதயாத் ॥

---

- Abugida (Indic)
- Languages – Tamil, Paniya, Saurashtra, Sanskrit
- People – Tamil, South Indian, Dravidian
- Places –Tamil Nadu, South India, Sri Lanka, Malaysia
- Related scripts – Brahmi, Pallava, Grantha, Kawi
- History – circa 600 BC to present. Official Language
- Unicode block U+0B80–U+0BFF, Supplement U+11FC0–U+11FFF

## 83. Telugu

ఓం భూర్ భువః స్వః

తత్ సవితుర్ వరేణ్యం

భర్గో దేవస్య ధీమహి

ధియో యో నః ప్రచోదయాత్ ॥

---

- Abugida (Indic)
- Languages – Telugu, Sanskrit, Gondi, Adivasi Oriya
- People – Telugu, South Indian, Dravidian
- Places –Andhra Pradesh, Telangana, South India
- Related scripts – Brahmi, Kadamba, Kannada
- History – circa 1300 AD to present. Official Language
- Unicode block U+0C00–U+0C7F

# 84. Tengwar (Elvish artificial language)

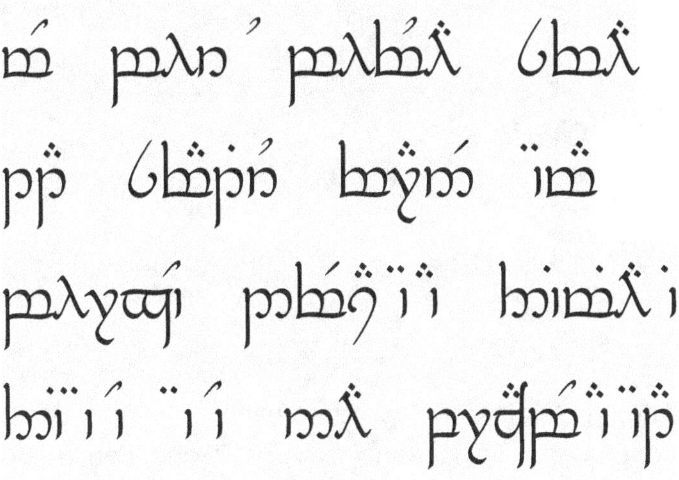

- Abugida (Artificial/Fictional)
- Languages – English, Elven fictional languages, i.e, Quenya, Telerin, Sindarin
- People – Elven
- Places –Middle Earth of J.R.R. Tolkien's novel
- Related scripts – Sarati & Valmaric fictional scripts
- History – circa 1300 AD to present. Official Language
- Unicode block – Private Use Area U+E000 to U+E07F

# 85. Thai

โอํ ภูรฺ ภุวห์ สฺวห์
ตตฺ สวิตุรฺ วเรณฺยมฺ
ภรฺโค เทวสฺย ธีมหิ
ธิโย โย นห์ ปฺรโจทยาตฺ

---

- Abugida (Mainland Southeast Asian)
- Languages – Thai, Lanna, Isan, Thai Song, Pali, Bisu
- People – Thai
- Places – Thailand, Laos, China
- Related scripts – Brahmi, Pallava, Khmer, Tai Viet
- History – circa 1283 AD to present
- Unicode block U+0E00–U+0E7F

# 86. Tifinagh (Berber)

ⴰⵓⵎ ⴱⵀⵓⵔ ⴱⵀⵓⵠⴰ ⵙⵠⴰⵀ

ⵜⴰⵜ ⵙⴰⵠⵉⵜⵓⵔ ⵠⴰⵔⴻⵏⵢⴰⵎ

ⴱⵀⴰⵔⴳⴰⵓ ⴷⴻⵠⴰⵙⵢⴰ ⴷⵀⵉⵎⴰⵀⵉ

ⴷⵀⵉⵢⴰⵓ ⵢⴰⵓ ⵏⴰⵀ ⵟⵔⴰⵛⴰⵓⴸⵢⴰⵜ

---

- Abjad (African)
- Languages – Tamazight, Amazigh, Zenaga, Berber, Numidian
- People – Berber
- Places – Morocco, Algeria, Tunisia, Canary Islands
- Related scripts – Egyptian hieroglyphs, Phoenician
- History – circa 3rd century BC to 3rd century AD
- Unicode block U+2D30–U+2D7F

# 87. Tibetan

ཨོཾ་བྷཱུར་བྷུཝཿ་སྭཿ

ཏཏ་སཝིཏུར་ཝརེཎྱམ྄

བྷརྒོ་དེཝསྱ་དྷཱིམཧི་

དྷིཡོ་ཡོ་ནཿ་པྲཙོདཡཱཏ་།

---

- Abugida (Indic), Languages – Tibetan, Sanskrit, Dzongkha, Ladakhi, Sikkimese, Ladakhi
- People – Tibetan, Places – Tibet, Nepal, Bhutan, India, Related scripts – Brahmi, Lepcha, Phags-pa
- History – circa 650 AD to present
- Unicode block U+0F00–U+0FFF

# 88. Tirhuta (Maithili)

𑓇 𑒦𑒴𑒩𑓂 𑒦𑒳𑒫𑓁 𑒮𑓂𑒫𑓁

𑒞𑒞𑓂 𑒮𑒫𑒱𑒞𑒳𑒩𑓂 𑒫𑒩𑒹𑒝𑓂𑒨𑒧𑓂

𑒦𑒩𑓂𑒑𑒼 𑒠𑒹𑒫𑒮𑓂𑒨 𑒡𑒲𑒧𑒯𑒱

𑒡𑒱𑒨𑒼 𑒨𑒼 𑒢𑓁 𑒣𑓂𑒩𑒔𑒼𑒠𑒨𑒰𑒞𑓂 ॥

---

- Abugida (Indic), Languages – Maithili, Sanskrit
- People – Bihari, Places – Bihar, Nepal
- Related scripts – Brahmi, Siddham, Odia
- History – circa 10th century AD to present
- Unicode block U+11480–U+114DF

## 89. Ugaritic cuneiform

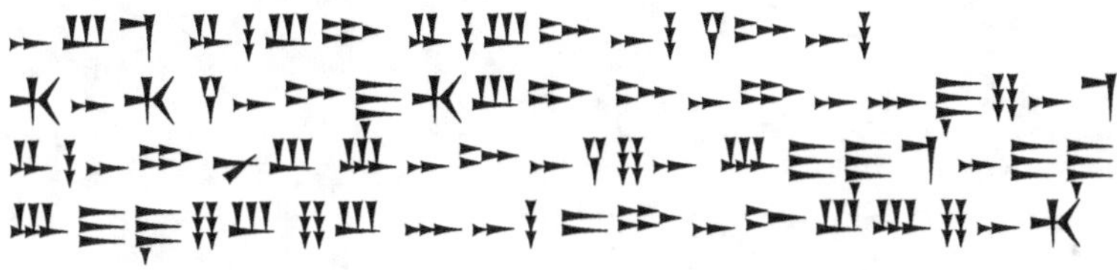

- Cuneiform (Middle Eastern), Languages – Ugaritic, Hurrian, Akkadian
- People – Syrian, Places – Syria
- Related scripts – Phoenician
- History – circa 1500 to 1200 BC
- Unicode block U+10380–U+1039F

## 90. Vai

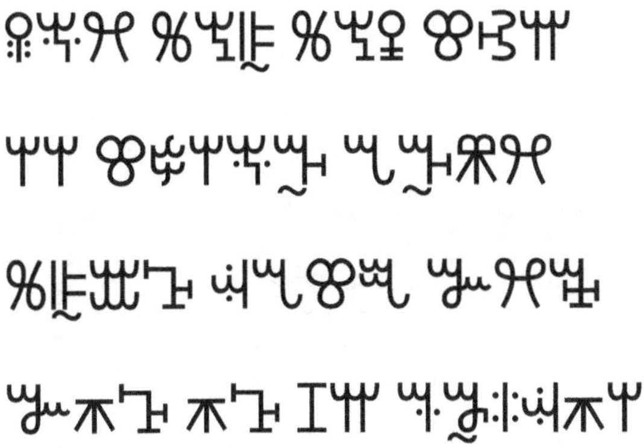

- Syllabary (African), Languages – Ugaritic, Hurrian, Akkadian
- People – Syrian, Places – Liberia, Sierra Leone
- Related scripts – Cherokee
- History – circa 1830 to present
- Unicode block U+A500–U+A63F

## 91. Vatteluttu (Tekken-Malayalam)

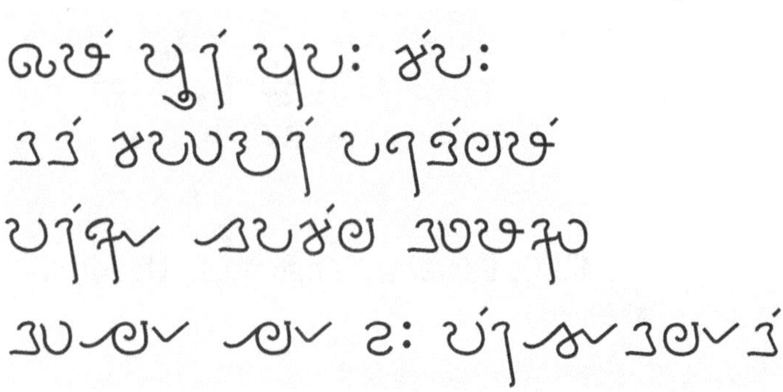

- Abugida (Indic), Languages – Tamil, Malayalam
- People – South Indian, Places – Tamil Nadu, Kerala, Sri Lanka, Related scripts – Brahmi, Pallava, Grantha
- History – circa 4th century to 8th century AD
- Unicode block - NONE

## 92. Wancho

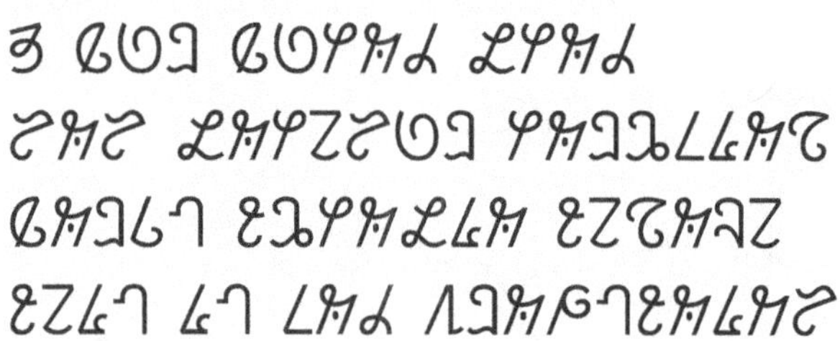

- Alphabet (Indic), Languages – Wancho
- People – Wancho, Places – Arunachal Pradesh
- Related scripts – NONE
- History – circa 2001 AD to present
- Unicode block U+1E2C0–U+1E2FF

## 93. Warang Citi (Barang Kshiti)

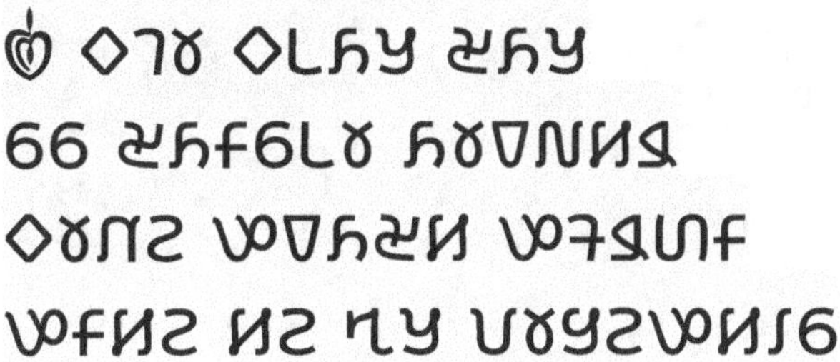

- Alphabet (Indic), Languages – Ho
- People – Ho, Munda tribal, Places – Jharkhand, Odisha, Bihar, Related scripts – NONE
- History – circa 1983 AD to present
- Unicode block U+118A0–U+118FF

## 94. Zanabazar Square (Mongolian)

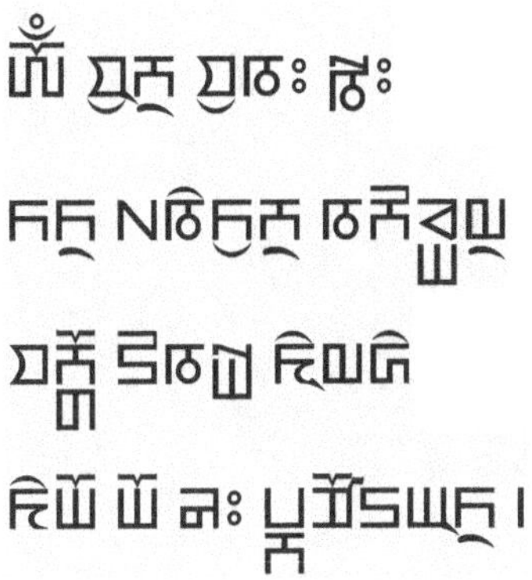

- Abugida (Central Asian), Languages – Mongolian, Sanskrit, Tibetan, **People** – Ho, Munda tribal, Places – Mongolia, Related scripts – Brahmi, Tibetan
- History – circa 1801 AD to 19th century
- Unicode block U+11A00–U+11A4F

## Scripts written RIGHT-TO-LEFT

## 95. Arabic

أم بحور بحفة سفاح تت
سأفتر فأرنيم
بحرج ديفزيا ذمه ضعيه يو
نه براشدياة

---

- Abjad (Middle Eastern)
- Languages – Arabic, Persian, Uyghur, Kurdish, Punjabi, Sindhi, Pashto, Urdu, Kashmiri, Somali
- People – Arabic, Middle Eastern
- Places – Saudi Arabia, UAE, Iraq, Iran, Pakistan, Afghanistan
- Related scripts – Phoenician, Aramaic, N'Ko
- History – circa 400 AD to present
- Unicode block U+0600-06FF, 0750-077F, 08A0-08FF, 0870-089F, FB50-FDFF, FE70-FEFF, 1EE00-1EEFF

# 96. Avestan

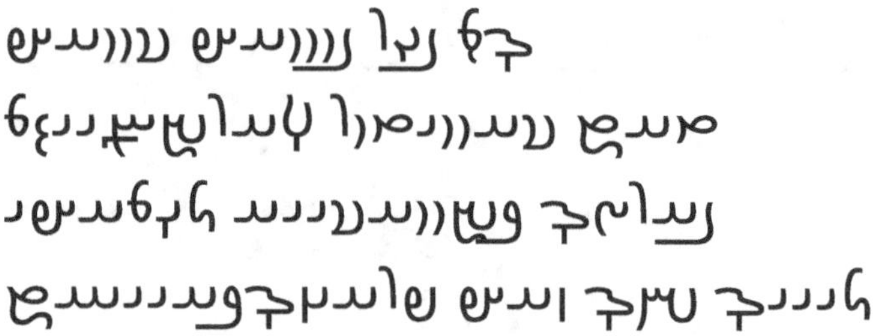

- Alphabet (Middle Eastern)
- Languages – Avestan, Middle Persian
- People – Iranian
- Places – Persia (Iran)
- Related scripts – Phoenician, Aramaic, Pahlavi
- History – circa 400 to 1000 AD
- Unicode block U+10B00 - U+10B3F

# 97. Hanifi Rohingya

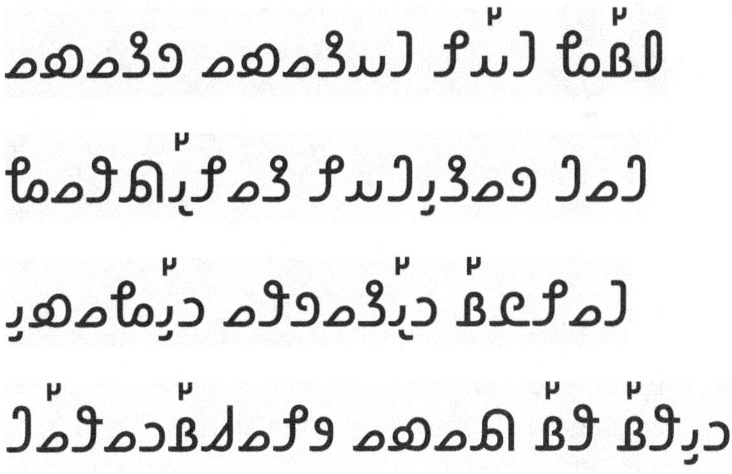

- Alphabet (Mainland Southeast Asian)
- Languages – Rohingya
- People – Rohingya
- Places – Myanmar, Bangladesh, Thailand
- Related scripts – Arabic, Urdu
- History – circa 1980 AD to present
- Unicode block U+10D00 - U+10D3F

# 98. Hebrew (Jewish)

אוֹם בּוּר בֱּבַס סְבַהַה
טַט סַבְטֶר וַרֶנְיַם
בַּרְגוֹא דֱבַסְיַה דְימַהּה
דְיוֹא יוֹא נַהַה פְּרַצ׳וֹדַיָט

---

- Abjad (Middle Eastern)
- Languages – Hebrew, Samaritan Aramaic, Yiddish, Tajik, Judeo Arabic, Ladino
- People – Jews, Arabs
- Places – Israel, Palestine
- Related scripts - Phoenician, Aramaic, Arabic
- History – circa 100 BC to present
- Unicode block U+0590 to U+05FF, Alphabetic Presentation Forms U+FB1D to U+FB4F

# 99. Lydian

𐤬𐤪 𐤡𐤰𐤭 𐤡𐤰𐤤𐤠 𐤮𐤤𐤠
𐤯𐤠𐤯 𐤮𐤠𐤤𐤦𐤯𐤰𐤭 𐤤𐤠𐤭𐤳𐤪𐤣𐤠𐤪
𐤡𐤠𐤭𐤸𐤬 𐤩𐤳𐤤𐤠𐤮𐤳𐤠 𐤩𐤦𐤪𐤠𐤦
𐤩𐤦𐤴𐤬 𐤴𐤬 𐤹𐤠 𐤡𐤭𐤠𐤨𐤬𐤩𐤦𐤠𐤯

---

- Alphabet (European)
- Languages – Lydian
- People – Rohingya
- Places – Manisa and Izmir inTurkey
- Related scripts – Phoenician, Anatolian
- History – circa 700 BC to 200 BC
- Unicode block U+10920 - U+1093F

# 100. Mandaic (Mandaean)

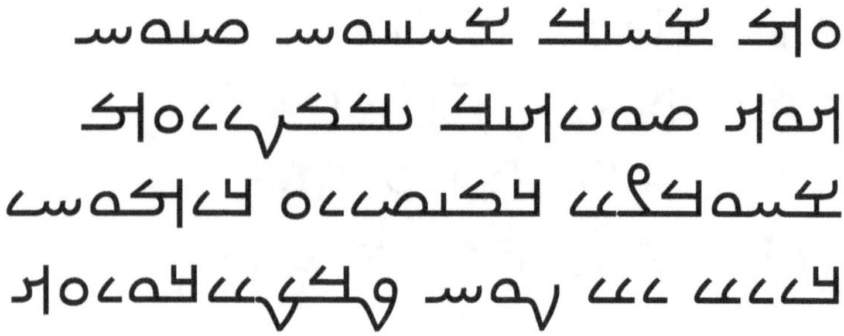

- Alphabet (Middle Eastern)
- Languages – Mandaic
- People – Mandaic
- Places – Iraq
- Related scripts – Phoenician, Aramaic
- History – circa 2nd century to 7th century AD
- Unicode block U+0840 - U+085F

# 101. N'Ko

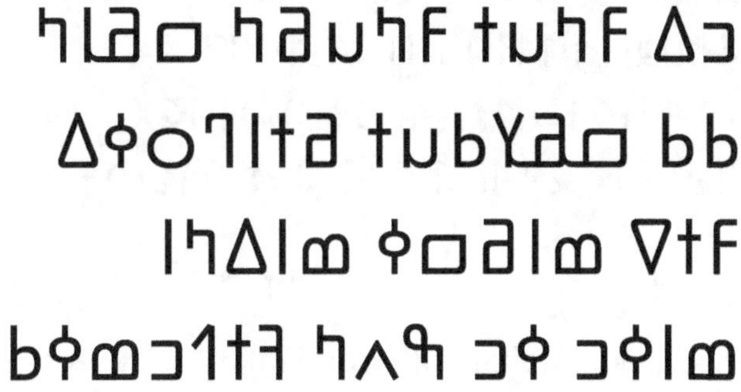

---

- Alphabet (African)
- Languages – N'Ko, Bambara, Kangbe, Jula
- People – Manding
- Places – Mali, Ivory Coast, Guinea
- Related scripts – Arabic
- History – circa 1949 AD to present
- Unicode block U+07C0 - U+07FF

# 102. Old Hungarian (Hungarian runes)

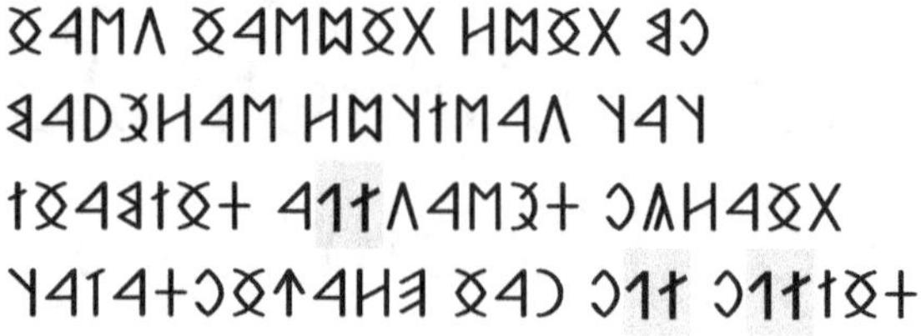

- Alphabet (European)
- Languages – Uralic
- People – Hungarian, Magyars
- Places – Hungary, Slovakia, Ukraine
- Related scripts – Phoenician, Syriac, Kharosthi
- History – circa 12th century to 17th century AD
- Unicode block U+10C80 - U+10CFF
- https://oldhungarian.eu/index_en.html

# 103. Samaritan

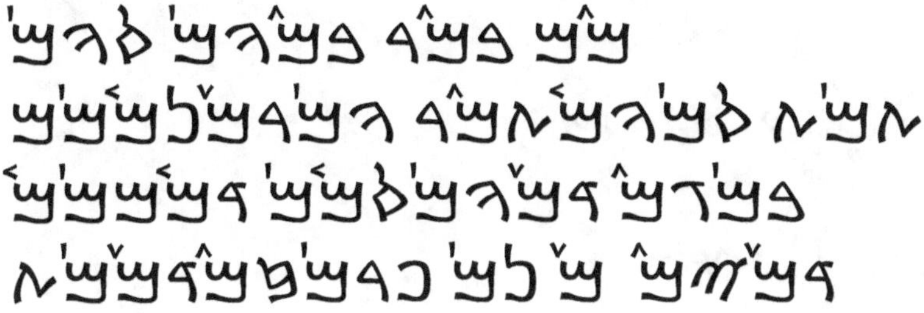

- Abjad (Middle Eastern)
- Languages – Samaritan Hebrew, Samaritan Aramaic, Arabic
- People – Samaritans
- Places – Israel, Palestine, West Bank
- Related scripts – Egyptian hieroglyphs, Phoenician, Paleo-Hebrew
- History – circa 600 BC to present
- Unicode block U+0800–U+083F

# 104. Thaana

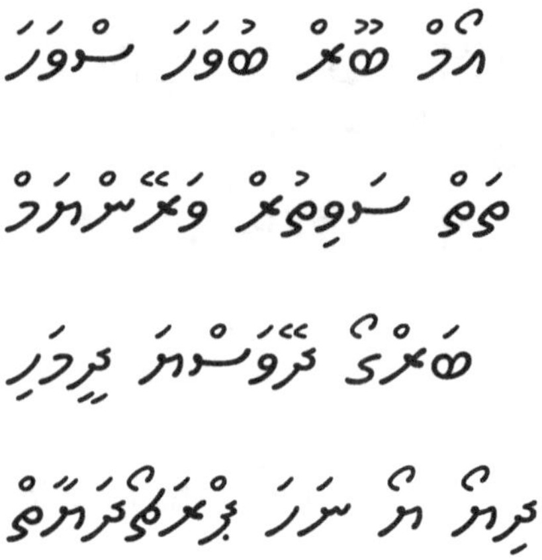

- Alphabet (Indic)
- Languages – Maldivian (Dhivehi), Mahl
- People – Maldivian
- Places – Maldives, Lakshadweep India
- Related scripts – Devanagari, Arabic
- History – circa 18th century AD to present
- Unicode block U+0780–U+07BF

# 105. Urdu

اومْ بھُورْ بھُوَہ سْوَہ تَتْ سَوِتُرْ وَرینْیَمْ
بھَرْگو دیوَسْیَ دھِیمَہِ دھِیو یو نَہ پْرَچودَیاتْ ۔

---

- Abjad (Indo-Iranian)
- Languages – Urdu, Punjabi
- People – Punjabi, Iranian, Pakistani
- Places – Iran, Pakistan, Afghanistan, , Punjab, Delhi
- Related scripts – Aramaic, Arabic, Persian
- History – circa 13$^{th}$ century AD to present
- Unicode block U+0600-06FF, 0750-077F, 08A0-08FF, 0870-089F, FB50-FDFF, FE70-FEFF

## Scripts written TOP-TO-BOTTOM

# 106. Mongolian (Qudum Mongyol bicig)

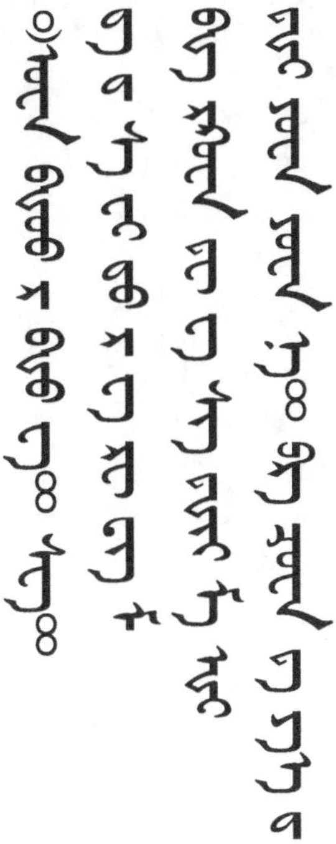

- Alphabet (Central Asian)
- Languages – Mongolian, Oirat, Manchu, Daur
- People – Mongol
- Places – Mongolia, China
- Related scripts – Phoenician, Syriac, Old Uyghur
- History – circa 1204 AD to present
- Unicode block U+1800–U+18AF, Supplement U+11660–U+1167F

# 107. Phags-pa (Mongolian square script)

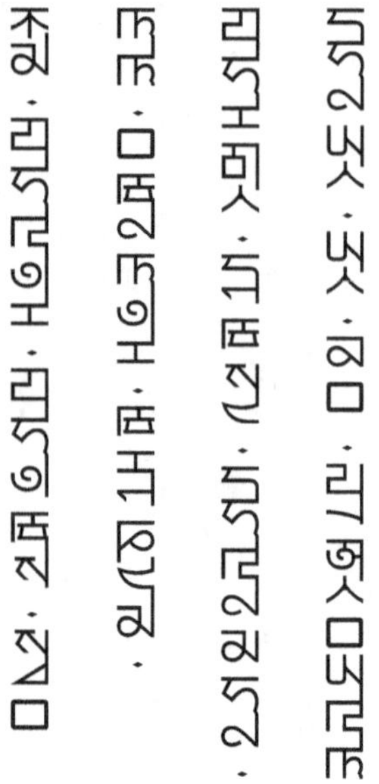

---

- Abugida (Central Asian)
- Languages – Mongolian, Tibetan, Chinese, Persian, Sanskrit, Uyghur
- People – Mongol
- Places – Mongolia, China
- Related scripts – Phoenician, Brahmi, Tibetan, Lepcha
- History – circa 1269 to 1360 AD
- Unicode block U+A840–U+A87F

# Scripts written BOTTOM-TO-TOP

# 108. Ogham (Irish Gaelic)

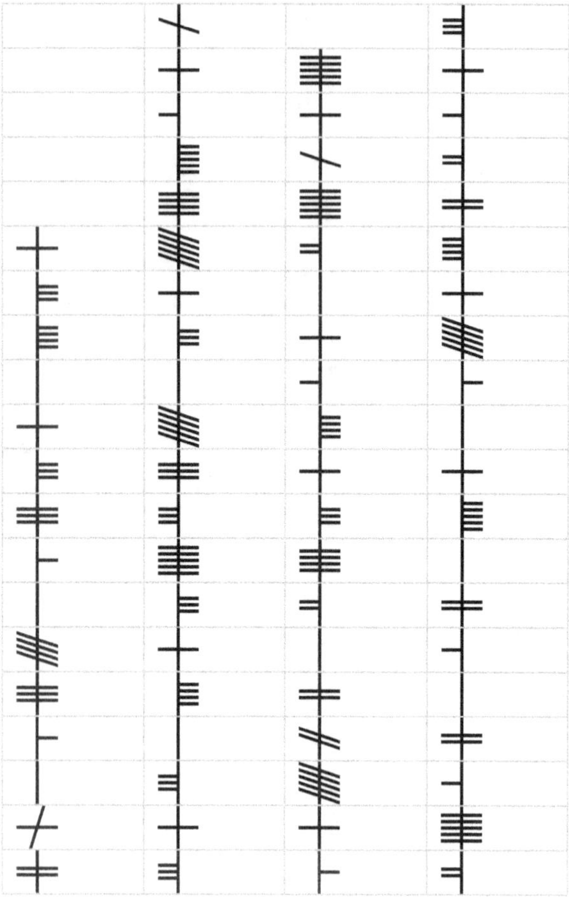

- Alphabet (European)
- Languages – Old Irish, Pictish
- People – Irish, Scottish
- Places – Ireland, England, Wales, Scotland
- Related scripts – Latin
- History – circa 5th century to 10th century AD
- Unicode block U+1680–U+169F

# Latin Transliteration Chart IAST

International Alphabet of Sanskrit Transliteration (IAST)

https://www.lonweb.org/links/sanskrit/lang/004.htm
https://en.wikipedia.org/wiki/International_Alphabet_of_Sanskrit_Transliteration

| a | ā | i | ī | u | ū | r̥ | r̥̄ | l̥ | |
|---|---|---|---|---|---|---|---|---|---|
| अ | आ | इ | ई | उ | ऊ | ऋ | ॠ | ऌ | |
| e | ai | o | au | ṃ | m̐ | ḥ | | oṃ | |
| ए | ऐ | ओ | औ | ◌ं | ◌ँ | ◌ः | | ॐ | |
| Consonants are shown with vowel 'a= अ' for uttering | | | | | | | | | |
| ka | क | ca | च | ṭa | ट | ta | त | pa | प |
| kha | ख | cha | छ | ṭha | ठ | tha | थ | pha | फ |
| ga | ग | ja | ज | ḍa | ड | da | द | ba | ब |
| gha | घ | jha | झ | ḍha | ढ | dha | ध | bha | भ |
| ṅa | ङ | ña | ञ | ṇa | ण | na | न | ma | म |
| ya | य | ra | र | la | ल | va | व | | |
| śa | श | ṣa | ष | sa | स | **Consonant only** | | | |
| ha | ह | | | | क्अ = क = ka , क् = k | | | | |

## International Phonetic Alphabet (IPA)

Some sample **IPA** sounds corresponding to the Sanskrit Devanagari and Latin IAST.

| अ a | आ ā | इ i | ई ī | उ u | ऊ ū |
|---|---|---|---|---|---|
| ə | aː | i | iː | ʊ | uː |
| ए e | ऐ ai | ओ o | औ au | अं aṃ | अः aḥ |
| eː | əi | oː | əu | | |
| क ka | ख kha | ग ga | घ gha | ङ ṅa | |
| kə | kʰə | gə | gʱə | ŋə | IPA |
| च ca | छ cha | ज ja | झ jha | ञ ña | |
| tʃə | tʃʰə | dʒə | dʒʱə | ɲə | IPA |
| ट ṭa | ठ ṭha | ड ḍa | ढ ḍha | ण ṇa | |
| ʈə | ʈʰə | ɖə | ɖʱə | ɳə | IPA |
| त ta | थ tha | द da | ध dha | न na | |
| t̪ə | t̪ʰə | d̪ə | d̪ʱə | nə | IPA |
| प pa | फ pha | ब ba | भ bha | म ma | |
| pə | pʰə | bə | bʱə | mə | IPA |
| य ya | र ra | ल la | व va | | |
| jə | ɹə | lə | ʋə | | IPA |
| श śa | ष ṣa | स sa | ह ha | | |
| ʃə | ʂə | sə | ɦə | | IPA |

https://en.wikipedia.org/wiki/IPA_vowel_chart_with_audio
https://en.wikipedia.org/wiki/IPA_pulmonic_consonant_chart_with_audio

## Script Types

Scripts or Written languages are classified as:

- Abugida - a writing system wherein every **Consonant letter** contains an inherent vowel, and the Consonant ligature gets modified by a diacritic when used with another vowel. Independent Vowels are also present, and tones and accents and special symbols.
- Alphabet - a written character represents a letter
- Abjad – a script with only consonants where vowels are implicit or optional
- Cuneiform – a mix of logographic and syllabary.
- Logographic – a written character represents a word or idea, i.e., a meaningful sound
- Syllabary - a written character represents a syllable, i.e., a distinct sound

## Language Families

Some of the main language families that categorize the spoken languages and their scripts in the world:

- Indo-European, Indo-Aryan, Indo-Iranian
- Sino-Tibetan
- Dravidian
- Austronesian
- Afroasiatic
- Germanic
- Slavic
- Turkic
- Semitic
- Italic

## Accented Gayatri Mantra

As seen in the Rigveda 3.62.10, we find accents used. These accents highlight pitch and sandhi during enunciation and increase the vibration quality of the chanting. Detailed explanation is in the Vajasaneyi Samhita of Shukla Yajurveda 36.3, along with the prefixed verse.

Note:
स्वः or सुवः? South Indian Krishna Yajurveda enunciation is सुवः and Shukla Yajurveda North Indian tradition chants it as स्वः ।

ॐ भूर् भुव॒स् स्व॑ः ।
तत् स॑वि॒तुर् वरे᳚ण्यं॒ भर्गो᳚ दे॒वस्य॑ धीमहि ।
धियो॒ यो न॑ः प्रचो॒दया᳚त् ॥

https://www.youtube.com/watch?v=aW_M7U-6KE0
https://www.sathyasai.org/devotional/gayatri
http://audio.awgp.org/album/play/31_gayatri_mantra
https://vedapurana.org/single.php?s=311&word=Gayatri_Mantra&secure
https://en.wikipedia.org/wiki/Gayatri_Mantra
https://www.svtsydney.org/wp-content/uploads/DownloadForms/Gayatri-Mantra-MV.pdf

## References

https://www.ashtangayoga.info/philosophy/sanskrit-and-devanagari/transliteration-tool/

https://en.wikipedia.org/wiki/International_Phonetic_Alphabet
https://www.newworldencyclopedia.org/entry/Devanagari
https://www.londonschool.com/blog/phonetic-alphabet/
https://www.internationalphoneticalphabet.org/ipa-sounds/ipa-chart-with-sounds/

https://software.sil.org/gentium/
https://translate.yandex.com/
http://aksharamukha.appspot.com/converter

https://scriptsource.org/cms/scripts/page.php?item_id=script_overview

https://www.unicode.org/iso15924/
https://unicode.org/iso15924/iso15924-codes.html

https://www.google.com/get/noto/
https://fonts.google.com/noto/fonts
https://notofonts.github.io/noto-docs/specimen/NotoSans/

https://omniglot.com/conscripts/index.htm
https://www.translitteration.com/what-is-transliteration/en/
https://www.lexilogos.com/keyboard/

Audio Chant of Gayatri Mantra
Anuradha P. https://www.youtube.com/watch?v=BwUcp7dSCK8
Pt. Jasraj https://www.youtube.com/watch?v=C6z2XV8G-oc
Shemaroo B. https://www.youtube.com/watch?v=O0SAgW9JBz4

## Epilogue

When one stops still and listens, a sound is heard. Felt within. Perhaps it is that Om, the un-struck without origin.

सर्वे भवन्तु सुखिनः । सर्वे सन्तु निरामयाः ।

सर्वे भद्राणि पश्यन्तु । मा कश्चिद् दुःख भाग् भवेत् ॥

ॐ शान्तिः शान्तिः शान्तिः ॥

When faith has blossomed in life,
Every step is led by the Divine.

Sri Sri Ravi Shankar

**Om Namah Shivaya**

जय गुरुदेव

www.ingramcontent.com/pod-product-compliance
Lightning Source LLC
Chambersburg PA
CBHW062142160726
48282CB00027B/912
* 9 7 8 9 3 9 2 2 0 1 2 6 4 *